One Girl in Auschwitz

Sara Leibovits, Eti Elboim

Producer & International Distributor
eBookPro Publishing
www.ebook-pro.com

One Girl in Auschwitz
Sara Leibovits, Eti Elboim

Translation from the Hebrew by Esther Frumkin
Poems by Sara Leibovits

Contact: eti.elboim@gmail.com
ISBN 9798587179820

ONE GIRL IN AUSCHWITZ

SARA LEIBOVITS
ETI ELBOIM

Auschwitz is a gaping hole in humanity's conscience, one that can be filled only by increasing light and goodness in the world.

One Girl in Auschwitz

This book is a story of rescue, of survival,
Of faith in the Creator of the World and in miracles, of man's
faith in himself,
Of courage, of heroism, of ingenuity, of strength, of
friendship,
Of caring, of seeking humanity even in the most difficult
moments,
Of seeking the light in the dark depths of suffering and
humiliation,
Of seeking the good in the world within a Hell of evil.
This is a story of the triumph of good over evil.

This story is insane, the stuff of nightmares, lacking human
logic, lacking humanity.
This story — is the naked truth.
It is what happened to me during one year of my life,
As a sixteen-year-old girl in Auschwitz.
This story is part of me, the only survivor of my entire family.
This story belongs to the entire Jewish people, and to all of us.

I hope that you come out of it stronger, with deeper faith,
Loving life more, understanding your purpose better,
Battling hatred, evil, arrogance, and racism,

Seeking goodness, compassion,
Helping others, kindness.
Love of another human being simply because he is human.
I survived in order to be able to testify and tell the story, and
here is my story.

Sara Leibovits of the Hershkovits family - Born in Czechoslovakia,
citizen of Israel

Daughter of the Girl in Auschwitz

This is the story of my mother, survivor of Auschwitz,
And it is also our story, second generation after the
Holocaust.
We were privileged to be born to those charred branches,
shadowed and smoking,
Those phoenixes that emerged from the fires of the cremato-
rium to be born anew.
They themselves embodied the vision of the dry bones,
Spread their wings and built families and homes.
For our sakes they learned anew how to laugh, how to be
happy,
How to become fit for happiness, for life.

Some of us carry in our souls cuts and scars,
But we have strength, power, and inspiration.
We are stronger than the inferno, more powerful than the
terror,
And our feet are planted firmly in the soil of our homeland,
the Land of Israel.
We drank the power and the memory of the Holocaust with
our mothers' milk.
The memory entered our bloodstreams with our father's every
caress and embrace.

We have the privilege of being a link in the chain
Between the survivors and the whole world.
They survived in order to tell the story,
And we are here to help them make their voices heard,
To tell, to speak, to document and to publicize,
To remind and protect so that it will never happen again!
We have promised that we will not let the world forget.

Eti Elboim of the Leibovits family, Born in Israel, Citizen of Israel

LAST STOP: AUSCHWITZ

The train slowed and then ground to a halt with a deafening screech of brakes. It was Thursday morning, May 18, 1944. Since Monday we were closed up in a boxcar, crowded together in darkness, filth, and hunger. Our travel companions were tears, anguish, and the terror of the unknown.

Now we huddled together and waited apprehensively for the locked doors of the car to be opened. Some of us had expressed the opinion that nothing good could come of traveling in a freight train, in cars that were normally used to transport livestock from Poland to Germany. And I thought to myself that perhaps even the animals were transported in more comfortable conditions than we, human beings, and that if this was the journey – what did it say about the place we had arrived at?

And even so, I had a faint hope that perhaps the situation would improve for my father, my mother, for my five younger brothers, for me, and the rest of the Jews who had traveled with us in the train. What more could a young girl ask for? I was 15 years and 10 months old. Suri Hershkovits, from the village of Komjat[1], which had been part of Czechoslovakia when I was

---

1   Komjat: Today this village is part of the Ukraine. It is called Velikiye
     Komyaty.

born there, but which had been annexed to Hungary on the eve of the war.

We had entered the freight car three days earlier, straight from the Munkács Ghetto, which itself had been Hell on Earth. We didn't yet know that small Hells awaited us during the journey towards a larger, ongoing Hell.

The entrance to the boxcar had no steps. The younger ones climbed up and jumped inside on their own, and the older ones were given a helping hand by those who were already inside.

When I got into the car, I was shocked to find that it was filthy and stinking from the cattle that had been transported in it before us. The floor was wet and dirty. It appeared that someone had made an attempt to wash it before we entered, but because they had rushed us in before it had time to dry, the floor was immediately covered with a sticky paste of mud and filth.

The first thing we noticed was that the car had no seats. Everyone had to stand, pressed against each other.

They told us not to be unruly and to behave ourselves. They explained that the car doors would be locked from the outside and would remain so until we arrived at our destination. Only "there" would the doors be opened because only "there" were the people who had the key. Where was "there?" We didn't know. We had no idea where we were headed.

As we were getting on the train, my cousin Shoni Salomon was appointed the commander of the car. I have no idea who appointed him to the position; I only remember that he was responsible. He was 19, from the neighboring village of Bogrovitch, the son of my father's sister Faige.

In one corner of the car children were crying, while in another corner people were trying to help some elderly passengers sit down on the floor. We were all terribly hungry and tired, which only increased the suffering. Our fellow passengers included mothers who had boarded the train alone with their children. In general, most of the people in the car were women, old people, children, and youths. There were very few men, because in those days most young men had been forcibly drafted into the Hungarian army. They were conscripted for hard labor, and after the German occupation they were taken prisoner. Thus, in addition to missing them, their families feared for their safety.

All together in the rail car we were 84 people, all terrified, strangers to each other. We were a random collection of people facing a common fate.

The next thing we noticed was that there was no drinking water in the freight car. We couldn't possibly imagine how we were expected to manage without water to drink.

For the first quarter-hour of the trip, we all tried to be polite and considerate. "Could you please move over a little," was heard from one direction. "Please, make a little space here," was heard from another. But then it became clear that the car also lacked toilets! We began to lose hope. Half an hour into our journey, the trip had already become torture.

My father called out, "Excuse me, does anyone have a blanket?" My father, Jacob Hershkovits, was 44 years old. Having served as the sexton of the synagogue, he was used to leading the community, and he helped his nephew, Shoni, take command of the car. The verse from *Ethics of the Fathers*, "In a place where there are no men, strive to be a man," applied to my father perfectly. He proved that even in the most difficult times, a person can show his humanity and help others.

Someone rummaged through his belongings and donated a wool blanket. "Excuse me," my father called again. "Does anyone have a hammer? A nail? A bucket?"

Somehow or other, without hammer or nails, my father and Shoni managed to hang up the blanket in a corner of the rail car to create a private toilet stall. But what to do with the bucket that was rapidly filling up to overflowing?

"The bucket has to be emptied outside," said one of the men. Someone suggested climbing on someone else's shoulders, grabbing the full bucket, and dumping its contents through the metal bars blocking the window. However, all the attempts to dump the bucket of waste outside, as the train rushed on, failed again and again.

"Does anyone have a newspaper?" my father and Shoni asked, hoping to be able to channel the contents of the bucket outside the window.

No one had a newspaper, however, and the car grew filthier and filthier, with a horrible stench. The train stopped at stations from time to time and each time we thought that perhaps we would receive water and be able to get rid of the stench in the car, but the doors remained locked for three full days.

Occasionally the train would wait at a station, sometimes for a short time and sometimes for much longer, perhaps to allow trains to change tracks. At some of the stations, good people who lived in the area were waiting for us, and they would throw us loaves of bread or boiled corn cobs through the bars. Everyone grabbed the food, and it was always gone within minutes.

Every time the train stopped at a station, we were all silent, trying to hear what language was being spoken outside, but usually they didn't allow people to come near the cars so we were left in ignorance.

The train journey took place amid sobbing and screaming. People dozed off standing and sitting. Every once in a while those standing would change places with those sitting, but there was never a moment of peace or calm in the car.

We were constantly trying to guess in which direction we were traveling. We couldn't see the sun, or the moon, or the stars. It seemed as though all of nature and the whole world was against us.

The windows were narrow, and when someone lingered near a window, everyone would immediately yell at him to get away from it so he wouldn't block the flow of air for everyone else. One time, when someone nevertheless managed to catch a glimpse of the landscape rushing by, he announced, "We're in Poland!"

My father also looked out the window and confirmed, "We're in Poland."

It is hard for a person to believe that he is being sent to death for no fault of his own, without any rational reason. The human mind cannot grasp this. This is perhaps why, despite the bone-shaking train journey, we had hope and we were optimistic.

When they first dragged us from our homes, the rumor had already spread among the Jews that we were being sent across the Danube River to a place called "Dona-tul" ("Across the Danube" in Hungarian), where standing water created black peat. My father and our neighbors discussed among themselves that apparently they were bringing all the Jews to this place so that we would drain the water from the soil and develop an advanced form of agriculture. My father and his friends were sure that we would succeed at the task. Today I know that during that period, each day four transports left Hungary, each one with about 3,000 Jews. In total, there were 147 transports carrying about 450,000 Hungarian Jews. In the preceding months, we had experienced anti-Semitism, endured suffering and hardships in the Munkács Ghetto, and had heard that in Ukrainian villages Jews had been taken out to pits to be shot, but if someone had told the travelers on our train, "Listen, most of you will die within an hour of your arrival at the final stop," we would have looked at him as though he had lost his mind.

Occasionally unpleasant clashes occurred during that train ride. One took place when a 14-year-old boy tied his shoes to the window bars by their laces. With the swaying of the train, the shoes came loose from the bars and fell, striking my mother in the face. They were shoes with metal buckles. My mother was struck in the eye and began to cry. My father examined the wound, gave her a handkerchief and reassured her that the situation wasn't so bad and that by the next day any sign of the blow would be gone. But people in the car immediately got up and turned on the boy in anger, wanting to hit him. My father felt sorry for him and tried to calm everyone down and make peace. He said to the angry crowd, "Let me handle the boy. I know how to educate children." With great difficulty he managed to stop the other travelers from thrashing the boy, who was the only son of a widowed mother. For the rest of the journey, my father continued to protect him from being hurt by the other travelers. My mother recovered, although her eye remained bruised and swollen.

The journey was terrible beyond description, but no one in our car died. At the end of the journey we stood, 84 people, nervously waiting for the car doors to open.

ARRIVAL AT AUSCHWITZ

The wait for the doors to open seemed endless to me. People tried to silence each other: "Shhh. . . Shhh. . . Let us hear what they're saying out there, and in which language!" But we couldn't hear a word outside the car. We had no idea where we were.

Suddenly the doors opened with a screech of hinges and we heard voices speaking German. A burst of fresh air flowed into the car, mingled with the thick air inside, reaching my nostrils, and filling my lungs. A ray of sunlight made its way through to me, over people's heads, and I saw that a beautiful, clear day awaited us outside. Where did such a beautiful, sunny morning come from?

Boys of 14 or 15 dressed in blue and gray striped prisoners' uniforms wearing identical cloth caps, climbed into the car. They urged us to get out, saying, "Don't take anything with you. Leave all your things here."

My mother told my brothers and me, "Children, quickly put on three shirts, because we have to leave everything here, but whatever is on you – that you're taking." She helped us all take clothing out of our bundles and put it on.

The youths hurried us out, not allowing us to linger in the car. They refused to say anything, as though they had been commanded not to talk to us about the place we had arrived at. The only thing they said was, "Get out! Get out!"

My father caught one of them in a corner of the car, placed his hands on the boy's shoulders, and asked him to tell him what this place was. The youth said something to my father. It seems that he told the truth, because up until that point my father had been telling us and the rest of the passengers to dress warmly and take bread, whoever had any, in our pockets. But after he spoke with the youth, he acted differently, saying quietly, "No need to take anything. We'll get out and they'll bring everything later."

Someone asked my father, "How will they know which bundle is mine?" I have no idea what my good father was thinking at that moment, what he was going through. Even if he knew that we had arrived at a place where they were killing Jews, there was not a single thing he could do, certainly not organize a rebellion or escape. Most of those present were women, children, and old people, sick, frail and weak. Not one of us could have rebelled or escaped. I assume that was why my father hid from my mother and the rest of the passengers the terrible secret that the youth had disclosed to him.

Since the car had no steps, we didn't know how to get out. The young people jumped to the ground, but the older people, pregnant women, and women holding onto small children had a hard time getting down. Some fell, and getting down from the train was difficult for most of us.

We were filthy, stinking, hungry, and weak. And even so, we still had hope that perhaps we had arrived at a place where people were waiting for us – the sky was blue, the sun shone cheerfully, we saw trees and grass, and we hoped that we had reached a beautiful, respectable place, and that in a little while we would bathe, eat, and become human beings again. We didn't imagine that we had arrived in Hell. We didn't know that within half an hour only a few of us would be left alive.

My mother, Blima Hershkovits from the Gelb family, born in the village of Komjat, was 38; my sister Rachel was 14, my brother Eliezer was 12, my brother Yosef Shalom 10, my sister Faigele 8, and my little brother Azriel Tzvi 3. Our sister Pessy had died four years earlier, at the age of nine months.

As we were getting down from the car, my mother was very concerned about a wound that my sister Ruchi had on her leg. Ruchi had gotten hurt in the Munkács Ghetto, and during the three-day train ride the wound had gotten infected and her leg had swelled up. My mother expected that we would get to a place where she could fill a basin with soap and water and soak the injured leg. She hoped that there would be a doctor or nurse who would give her some ointment.

Ruchi was taller than me and looked older than I did. When they wanted to tease me, they would tell me, "She's the oldest." We two were the best of friends. And in general, I loved all my younger siblings very much.

My mother was also bothered by the "shiner" on her eye, from the blow she received from the shoes in the railcar. She asked us, "Can you see the bruise?" She was a beautiful woman, with big green eyes, and it was important to her to look healthy and strong in this foreign place that we had come to. Perhaps she instinctively understood that in this place it was better not to look ill or wounded.

Five minutes after we got out of the train, we noticed someone standing at the end of the tracks, flanked by male and female soldiers. My brother said, "I see a man standing on a chair."

"Maybe because he is short," guessed my mother and stared straight ahead to see what was happening. None of us imagined that the man standing at the head of the soldiers, receiving the long line of those who had gotten off the train – sometimes Josef Mengele himself, and sometimes another Nazi officer -- would determine who would live and who would die. The man stood, a large stick in his hand, as though he were directing a satanic chorus that decided people's fate.

The air was filled with a strange smell that I couldn't identify in my first hour at Auschwitz. Smoke rose from a chimney up to the sky, and I didn't know what it meant.

They separated my father from us and took him to the side with other men.

Suddenly my mother began screaming the name of my 10-year-old brother, Yosef Shalom. The boy had disappeared in the swarm of people, and because of the tremendous crowding, it was impossible to find him. My mother called him in a panic, but my brother was nowhere to be found. Even today I still hope that they met up together later on.

We walked together with a long line of women and children; alongside us was another long line of men and teenagers. We were surrounded by sobbing and screaming. Soldiers stood along the sides holding the leashes of terrifying dogs that were waiting for their masters to release them and command them to attack us.

On both sides of us were high, barbed-wire fences, but we couldn't see the prisoners in this place, perhaps because at this hour they were closed up in their barracks.

When we reached the head of the line, a female soldier quickly came up to me and shoved me to the right.

My mother, who in her youth had studied in an Austro-Hungarian school in Komjat and spoke German, asked the soldier politely not to take me, since I was her daughter.

The soldiers lifted the butts of their rifles and were about to beat my mother. I begged, "Mama, it doesn't matter, just don't let them beat you." My mother agreed, saying, "Go, so they shouldn't beat you, too."

At the same time they took more people out of the line. Behind us was a family from Komjat with 10 children whose mother had died a month earlier. They separated out one of the older daughters, Ruchi Klein, who was 18 years old, from her younger siblings and took her to the right.

Ruchi began shouting at her younger siblings, "My orphans!"

My good mother saw that they were about to beat Ruchi and told her, "Ruchele, you go to the other side and watch over Suri for me, and I'll watch over your siblings." Immediately she gathered the little orphans around her and gave them her hand.

She even had time to turn her head to me and shout, "We'll see each other in the evening!"

Those were my mother's last words: "We'll see each other in the evening!"

SEVENTY YEARS LATER

As a second-generation Holocaust survivor, I went through the Holocaust in a different way at every age.

When I was a child I thought to myself – I would have jumped from the train, escaped through the narrow crack in the window, and I wouldn't have cared if I had cut my knee or broken my leg. I would have rolled over as I landed and would have run to the forest, joined the Partisans, lived with them, learned how to fight the Nazis, learned how to shoot a gun, and fought courageously for the right to be a human being and to live. I would not have gone to the gas chambers. No, no, they wouldn't have taken me there.

When I was 15 1/2, I thought to myself – I would have behaved like my mother, who was my age at the time. I would not have escaped from the train, because I would not have left my parents and younger siblings behind. I would not have been able to live with the knowledge that I had escaped and left them to their fate. I would have come to Auschwitz with my family and surely would have survived the initial selection. I would have spent my days in Auschwitz with courage, strength, and wisdom, like my mother did. I would have looked around me all the time with watchful, sharp eyes in every direction, ingeniously seeking ways to survive. I would not have given in to despair, or given up. I would have done anything necessary in order to survive. Or, on second thought, almost anything.

When I was 23 and my oldest son was placed in my arms for the first time, I thought to myself – If I were getting out of the train at this moment, the Nazis would surely have grabbed the infant from me and given him to one of the mothers to take him with the women and children marching forward. They would have pushed me to the side, with the group of women who had passed the selection, having been determined fit to work. But I would not have been capable of separating from my son. I would have slipped away and run to join the line of women and children marching towards the unknown. I would have rocked the infant in my arms and walked with him into the gas chamber. I would not have been able to stay alive knowing that my son had been murdered.

When I was 38, I thought to myself – now I am the age of my Grandma Blima Hershkovits, may God avenge her blood. She came to Auschwitz with six children. At that age I also had six small children.

After a decade and a quarter, I reached the age of 51 and thought to myself – my Grandma Sheindel Leibovits, may God avenge her blood, came to Auschwitz at this age, when she was the mother of 10 and grandmother of 4. The Nazis viewed both my grandmothers as older women, caretakers of children, who would not be able to serve the Nazi machine by performing physical labor, and therefore sent them immediately to the gas chambers. Perhaps, at my present age, they would have sent me there, too.

In every generation a person must see himself as though he were saved from Auschwitz.

FIRST HOURS IN AUSCHWITZ

The two lines, one of men and one of women, proceeded straight forward, and gradually moved away from us. I was left on the platform with the other women who had been taken out of the line. It seems to me that perhaps 1% of the people had been sent off to the right with me. I didn't know then whether it was a good thing or a bad thing. I hoped that we would meet again later on.

Around us were scattered thousands of bags and packages left orphaned outside the train cars. They commanded us to stand in lines of five girls each. We stood there and waited. I was famished, needed a toilet, and confused and filthy. Suddenly I saw my father. He stood together with the men who had been taken out of the main line, not far from me. I left my row and ran to him. He had a water bottle and gave me a little water to drink. Out of his bag he withdrew some bread and *schmaltz* (a spread of goose fat) that his sister Faige Solomon, Shoni's mother, had given him when he left the train. He dipped two slices of bread in the schmaltz and gave them to me. As I devoured the food, my hunger abated.

I returned to my place in the women's line. They led us away from the men's group, making us walk a distance of about two kilometers. The place looked enormous to me, and at that time I had not yet even learned its name.

At first we had difficulty walking in rows of five. Every once in a while someone would get confused and move to a different line, but when we realized that anyone who mixed up the marching order got a powerful slap, we rapidly learned to walk in fives and not stray from our rows.

We reached a bath house. Since I had eaten and drunk something, I was slightly more refreshed than I had been when we arrived. I was not particularly worried that they would do something bad to us, for I could not yet imagine that we had arrived at a genocide factory whose purpose was to destroy an entire people – an understanding too complex and satanical for the brain of a young girl. But as the oldest daughter, I worried in general about my family, about my sister Ruchi with the injured leg, and my brother Yosef Shalom, who had disappeared.

We were instructed to undress. We were told that each one of us would get a locker where we could put our clothes and belongings. Every locker had a number, and they asked us to remember the number and where our locker was located. All my possessions at that moment were the clothes I had on – three shirts, a green sweater that I had knitted myself, a skirt, socks, and shoes. I was wearing no jewelry, since all our jewelry had been taken while we were in the Munkács Ghetto.

The women in charge of us were themselves prisoners, Jews from Slovakia who had already been in Auschwitz for two to three years. They were tough, but at first they spoke to us politely.

We were left standing in our underwear, glancing at each other with embarrassment. At this stage the commanders' tough side took over, and they began beating us and screaming at us to strip completely. I felt as though the sky had fallen on me. I came from a home where we had comported ourselves modestly, and I had never seen anyone naked. I was in shock.

Once we had taken off all our clothes, we were commanded to stand in rows before five or six women to have our hair cut. When my turn came I stood before one of these women, who were also Jews. The woman, a long-time prisoner in Auschwitz, began shaving the hair off my head with an electric shaver. Like any teenage girl, I had spent a lot of time fixing my hair. My hair was then brown and straight, falling to my shoulders, combed with a side part. In that period, curly hair was in fashion, so every night I would fold papers, tie them into my hair, and pray to wake up the next morning with curly hair. My sister Ruchi had light hair that was naturally curly, and she had bangs. In the ghetto, Ruchi and I had already, to our great sorrow, parted with our long hair, making do with short hair, since the ghetto was infested with lice. But now this woman was going to shave my hair off completely! Bald? Me? I glanced to the right and to the left and realized that everyone was being shaved bald.

The electric shaver ran on batteries, and it stopped working in the middle of shaving my head. The woman picked up a pair of large scissors and finished cutting my hair roughly. She cut the back of the head and left it full of scratches and cut marks. Then they went on to remove the hair from all parts of our bodies. We were left naked, shorn, and humiliated.

Next we were herded into another room, where irrigation pipes punctured with holes were affixed to the ceiling and attached to a military water tank, serving as showers. The tank was heated, so the water was hot, but after a few minutes the water in the tank ran out. We were told that they had gone to bring another tank, and meanwhile we stood there for about two hours, naked, freezing, waiting for the water. Finally a new tank was hooked up and hot water was sprayed on us. Then we were given bars of soap that gave off a terrible smell. The commander told us that the soap was called "R.J.F.," an acronym for *reine* (clean), *judische* (Jewish), *fett* (fat). The women around me didn't understand what she was talking about. I didn't understand either. They made the soap out of human beings? Were they crazy?

All of us lathered ourselves with that soap. They forced us to.[2]

When the shower was finished, we stood and dried off in the air, without towels. Each of us received a gray dress made of a fabric that looked like sackcloth. All the dresses were the same size, made of one piece of fabric, without seams or a belt. Since I was short, my dress dragged on the floor. I was also given shoes that were too big for me. And thus, with a trailing dress and too-large shoes, I could barely walk.

The girls around me advised, "Suri, cut off the bottom of the dress," but no one had a pair of scissors.

---

2   Scholars currently hold that there was no soap made from human fat at Auschwitz. In fact, the soap bars in Auschwitz were stamped with the letters RIF, which can be mistaken as RJF. However, this is what we were told, and this is what shocked us then.

Someone else said to me, "When we get there, we'll take a stone and tear the bottom of the dress off." But there was no stone anywhere. The place was clean, scrubbed, sterile. I had no choice but to step on the dress with my big shoes.

Who would have believed that we would be wearing this garment, just as it was, for the next two weeks and two days straight, without changing our clothes even once in all that time?

FIRST NIGHT IN AUSCHWITZ

At the end of our first day in Auschwitz, they took us to "quarantine." They told us that we would remain in detention for two weeks to make sure that we didn't have any diseases.

On the way, men passed by us and yelled, "Where are you from?" They spoke Hungarian. One of them threw a piece of bread towards us, and it fell on the ground. The bread was black, from flour ground with the husk of the grain, baked in a square pan. I picked up the chunk of bread, but none of us wanted to eat bread like that. Someone whispered, "That's the only kind of bread they have here." So I didn't throw it away. Anyway, there was nowhere to throw it. On all sides, everything was perfectly clean. Not a piece of paper or a leaf could be seen on the ground.

At midnight we came to Block 13. They stood us in formation, in rows of five women, and carried out a selection. Anyone who did not seem suitable in the commanders' eyes was pulled out of line and taken away. I stood in formation with the black bread under my armpit. Since my dress was so large, they didn't notice it.

We stood in formation for about two hours. None of us had a watch, and my sense of time was completely blurred, so I don't know if we actually stood there for two hours or if it just seemed like that. From that day on, time became amorphous, undefined. Auschwitz time.

As we stood in formation, the commander told us that we were going into Block 13. They took one group of girls at a time and brought them inside. When it came time for my group to go in, the "*blokova*," director of the block, showed us the boards on which we were to sleep. She asked, "Do you know where you are?" I don't remember what we answered. And what could we have said? She instructed 14 women to climb onto one of the boards and go to sleep.

We lay there all together – seven women with their heads in one direction and seven with their heads in the other direction, with our legs between the other women's heads. I had never been in such a shocking situation in my life.

Someone asked the blokova where the pillows were, and received two slaps in reply.

When the blokova left, I pulled out the bread that I had hidden in my armpit. All the women around me asked for a piece. The thought that the bread had been thrown at us because it tasted bad quickly gave way to the understanding that this was the taste of the bread in this place. At this point we were famished.

Someone asked the blokova where she could wash her hands, and the answer was two powerful slaps. Even though I had grown up in an observant home and was not used to eating bread without first ritually washing my hands, I said the blessing over the bread with a heavy heart and ate it with unwashed hands.

The first night in Auschwitz was very bewildering. I had no idea where I was. We barely had time to lay our heads on the board and close our eyes when the blokova was already waking us up. She made us go outside for a roll call in order to memorize the way back to our board. Thus, several times in the course of that first night, we were made to leave our boards and go outside for roll call.

All of us had shaved heads and looked alike. We could scarcely identify each other. Once during that night, when someone climbed onto the board, a woman screamed, "A boy climbed on me!" She thought that the shaved girl was a boy.

There were several girls from our village, Komjat, with me in Block 13. Among them were Ruchi Klein, who had promised my mother that she would look after me; 22-year-old Sheyvi Avram, my mother's cousin, who was with me all the time in Auschwitz and later as well; her sister Idsko Avram, who was 14 but looked older; and four sisters from the Deutsch family – Yehudit (Yeidis), 26, Libu, 19, Mugda (Malka), who was my age and had studied with me in school, and Dina, who was a year younger than us. We all supported each other, and my one small comfort that first night was that at least a few of my friends were there with me.

The work managers in Auschwitz were called "*kapo*." Eventually I learned that the word "kapo" comes from Italian and means "head." The head of the block was called "*blokova*" or "*blokaltester*," which means "elder of the block." The blokova responsible for our block was named Gizi. She had deputies who were called "*shtubova*." "*Stube*" means "room" and "*ova*" means "hers;" in other words, they were the guardians of the room. The blokovas, shtubovas, and kapos were Jewish prisoners from Poland and Slovakia. They had been in Auschwitz for a long time before we got there, and they were part of a group of prisoners who had been given positions of authority, known as "prominent." By virtue of their jobs, they had better conditions, better food, and more privileges, which led many of them to be corrupt and cruel.

Gizi had a sister by the name of Lili, who was a shtubova. Lili was sickly, and Gizi, under the protection of her elevated position, took good care of her sister. The barracks held about 400 prisoners, and two shtubovas were in charge of each quarter of the barracks. The shtubovas didn't hesitate to scream, punish, or beat prisoners brutally.

Half-way through the first night they woke us up again and made us go outside for roll call. Suddenly Gizi identified her cousin, who had lived in our village, among the rows of girls. Four years earlier, at the beginning of the war, Gizi and Lili's parents, who lived in Slovakia, had sent their youngest son to Komjat to save him. By then we were already part of Hungary, and they believed that the Jews' situation in Hungary would be better than in Slovakia, and thus the boy would be saved. Now Gizi realized that if her cousin was here, it was a sign that her little brother, who was already 15, had arrived in Auschwitz, too. Her eyes bulged out of her head with rage. She grabbed her cousin, who was about 14, and began beating her brutally, screaming, "Is my brother here too? Idiots! Couldn't you have escaped?"

We stood by, frozen with terror. We didn't understand why

Gizi was hitting her cousin like that. Gizi continued screaming, "Idiots! Why didn't you escape?"

Tears ran down my cheeks and choked my throat. The girl was crying and trying to shield her head with her hands, but her cousin continued beating her brutally and shouting, "Aren't you ashamed to be here?"

I thought that perhaps Gizi was taking out on her cousin all her rage at being prisoner herself for three years.

I knew Gizi's brother, who had always dressed nicely. As far as I could recall, he had not been among the men who were pulled aside from the line. Apparently he had marched straight forward together with the mothers and children from our train. Today I understand that Gizi must have realized that her brother had been killed in Auschwitz and was angry that her family's attempts to save him had failed. She continued screaming and beating her cousin, until the girl was left lying unconscious on the floor. We never saw the poor girl again.

That was our first acquaintance with the Gizi the blokova. She was plump and walked with large steps. In her little room at the entrance to the block, she had a table covered with a cloth, and she used to prepare, for herself and her sister, tea and even coffee, which was a rare commodity during the war. When she prepared her drinks, all the women in the block would sniff enviously and sigh in sorrow.

SMOKE FROM THE CREMATORIUM

At the end of the first night, we were woken up very early in the morning. Bright light filtered through the tiny windows of the block. The first morning in Auschwitz. At the command of the shtubova who was screaming at us, I jumped off the board onto the floor, wondering if we would be changing our clothes now. About 400 prisoners were dressed in gray sackcloth dresses, and it didn't seem like anyone intended to arrange clean clothes for all of us. I had already figured out that no one in this place slept in a nightgown or pajamas, but it was hard for me to grasp that we were expected to go through an entire day wearing the clothes in which we had slept.

We asked each other, "Where is the water?" "Where are the toilets?" No one knew. The shtubovas yelled, "Go outside for roll call and stand in rows of five!" They lashed out in all directions with a whip made of leather strips. Anyone who took a wrong step or uttered an unnecessary word got lashed.

We stood in formation for about two hours. Meanwhile, the blokova and shtubovas took their time eating breakfast, until a female German officer arrived. Gizi and her shtubovas went out to the officer and began fawning over her.

They started to count us and then commanded, "Sit!"

We were amazed – sit on the bare dirt? With no grass and no blanket?

We sat there for several hours. Eventually they passed out mugs of a hot drink. I was the first one in our row of five, and I took the mug and sipped from it. A woman in another row noticed that the drink was greenish and gave off a strange odor. She started whispering, "Don't drink it, it's green. I read in a book that poison has a green color." We all looked at her in panic. I was sure that I had drunk poison and that I was going to die in another second. Suddenly it was clear to me that in this place they poisoned, murdered, and burned people. Everyone was watching me, asking, "Does it hurt?" "Are you nauseous?" "Do you feel sick?"

I felt awful. Along with everyone else, I waited for the moment when something would happen to me, but when some time passed and nothing at all happened, we understood that the drink was not poison. Apparently, that's just what tea at Auschwitz looked and smelled like.

At about 11:00 we were taken to the toilets. Until then, anyone who was unable to hold in her urine or feces took whip lashes on her face. When they brought us into the toilets, I was in shock. A long concrete strip, about 110 or 120 centimeters wide, had holes spaced about half a meter apart. We could not believe that human beings were being required to do their business in this way, without barriers between people, without seats, without water, and without paper. It was inhuman. Incomprehensible. We were commanded to sit down on the holes. Anyone who did not fulfill the command met a bitter fate. Thus they took control of our souls, our bodies, and our needs.

When we got back to the block, the women began asking the blokova and shtubovas, "Where is my mother?" "Where are my children?" "Where is our family?" The blokova said, "Do you see that smoke over there? That's not a bakery, like you thought, it's a crematorium. That smoke is your families."

None of us understood what she meant. We thought that she was just trying to scare us.

She said, "They were burned in that crematorium. You will never see them again, and you need to know that."

In the same breath, the blokova Gizi went on to explain the rules of the place to us. She explained that the roll call was called "*zahlappell*" ("*appell*" meaning call and "*zahl*" meaning number). Prisoners were counted every morning before going out to work, during work, and when they returned from work to the block.

As the day passed, the blokova's words about the crematorium haunted us. At first none of us could believe her. The women whispered to each other that the blokova and shtubovas just wanted to frighten us to avenge themselves for the suffering that they themselves had endured here. But gradually the understanding seeped into our brains and dripped into our hearts and souls. First one girl sobbed bitterly but quietly, "Oh my God, they've burned my mother, father, brother, sister, grandmother . . ." After her, someone else burst into tears, and then a third and a fourth. By the time the Sabbath came, we were all sobbing with the realization that they had murdered our families. I mourned deeply, and feared that I was the only member of my family left alive.

Now we also understood the meaning of the cries that we had heard on the first day. We had been standing in a big group, in rows of five girls, when we had suddenly heard sobbing. I had not identified the voices at the time, but someone insisted that she had heard calls of "*Sh'ma Yisrael.*[3]" Rumors began to spread among us that every day thousands of Jews were brought into shower stalls, but instead of being sprayed with water, they were sprayed with a gas that killed them. Their bodies were then burnt in the crematoria, and the smoke that rose every day from the chimneys was indeed their bodies being consumed and rising heavenward, just as Gizi had said. Hearing that was the most terrifying thing I had ever experienced in my life. I had found myself in a place more horrifying than I could ever have imagined.

MEMORIES OF MY BELOVED PARENTS

In the following days, I silently mourned the death of my family members. Before my eyes, I saw my father sitting at the Sabbath table, my mother serving her delicious dishes, whose taste I will remember forever, and my little brothers, with their sweet faces, sitting around the table and singing Sabbath songs with my father. My heart was torn with the knowledge of their murder. I couldn't grasp the thought that I would never see them again. I wanted someone to shake me and awaken me from this horrible dream.

At night, lying on the cold, hard board, before falling into a senseless stupor laced with sorrow, I would tell myself stories from home. Among them was the tale of how my mother and father met, one that I had loved to hear as a child.

My father, Jacob, was the eighth of nine children. My mother Blima was also the eighth of nine. That was the first thing they had in common. They lived in neighboring villages in the Carpathian region – my father in Bogrovitz and my mother in Komjat – but they had never met as young people.

My father was born in 1900 into the Hershkovits family, a well-off family that owned several forests. At the age of 14 his parents sent him to study in the well-known Galanta Yeshiva in Slovakia. His parents rented him a room in a widow's home and, like other yeshiva students in those days, he ate his evening meals with various Jewish families near the yeshiva, a custom known as "days."

The room my father rented in the widow's home had two beds, and the other bed was occupied by Shmaya Gelb, my mother's brother, four years her senior. My father and Shmaya got along very well and became good friends. My father's parents gave him money for food, in addition to the "days" meals, and every time he went to the bakery he would buy rolls for his friends as well, some of whom, including Shmaya, came from families who were just scraping by.

On the eve of every new month, his mother would send a servant to the yeshiva with a basket containing cakes and money for the coming month. On account of all the rolls he bought, it happened more than once that my father ran out of money before the end of the month.

Thus my father and Shmaya studied together for three years. When my father reached the age of 17, he transferred to a different yeshiva. Although it was then the middle of World War I, his wealthy parents had saved him from being drafted by paying a ransom to the army.

During the war, the financial situation of the Gelb family from Komjat deteriorated. Shmaya had to cut short his studies at the Galanta Yeshiva and return home to help support the family. Some of the Gelb children were married, and the family's financial situation continued to be difficult. My grandfather, Eliezer Gelb, was forced to relocate to America to support his family. He worked there as a teacher in a *cheder*[3], lived hand-to-mouth, and saved up money penny by penny. My grandfather asked my grandmother to pack up their possessions, collect all the unmarried children, and join him in the United States, but Grandma Chana-Devora refused to leave Komjat.

Three years later my grandfather returned from America with the money he had saved and opened a textile store in Komjat. Grandma was very talented and knew how to sew, and for a few years they ran a successful business together.

One day my grandfather went into the city to buy fabrics. When he was ready to return to the village, he ordered a coach and loaded the cart with the rolls of fabric. On the way, the driver got into an accident, and my grandfather fell from the cart and was killed. He was 56 when he died. My grandmother and her daughters waited for him all night, until they were notified of the tragedy early the next morning.

Everyone in the region heard about Eliezer Gelb's death. Everyone came to comfort the mourners, including my father, then 23 years old, who came to comfort his good friend Shmaya. The moment he entered the house of mourning, my father noticed his friend's sister, Blima, a beautiful 17-year-old girl of good character, and fell in love with her at first sight. The next day he began courting my mother, sending the Gelb family an enormous basket of fruits and vegetables. On that Friday he sent a servant bearing cakes and challahs. The widow and her daughters asked about the young man who was sending

---

3   *cheder*: A school at which kindergarten- and elementary-school-aged children learn Torah.

them food, and Shmaya revealed to my grandmother that it was his good friend from yeshiva, and that he was courting Blima. When my father next came to visit, my grandmother saw a nice-looking man with brown eyes, dimples, good manners, and a ready smile. He was also learned, quick-witted, energetic, wealthy, and respected.

The families began to discuss marriage. They asked Shmil Avram from Bogrovitz, who was related to both sides (and also a relative of Sheyvi Avram, my friend from Komjat who was with me in Auschwitz), to negotiate the marriage terms. My mother had virtually no dowry, since the merchandise had been stolen from the cart after the accident, leaving the Gelb family penniless. But my father was not interested in a dowry, and he and my mother became engaged anyway.

My parents were married in 1925, and I was born three years later. My Hebrew name is Sarah. My Czech name was Sarena, and that is what I was called at school. When my Czech teachers and friends wanted to use an affectionate nickname, they called me Sarenka. My family and Jewish acquaintances called me Suri or Suriko.

My mother and father were very much in love, and my father always had a good word for my mother. On Sabbath eves my father would say to us, "So, children, tell me the truth. Didn't I choose a good mother for you?"

My mother was talented at handiwork, like her mother, Chana-Devorah, and she embroidered and crocheted large lace curtains that hung in our living room, as well as table-cloths, napkins, pillows, and sheets. Every time my mother was complimented on her beautiful work, my father would say gently, "So what did you expect? Mother is very talented."

My father played the violin. As a child he learned to play from gypsies who played at Jewish weddings. They lived at the foot of the mountain on whose slopes the village of Bogrovitz was located, and my father would go down the mountain to their camp and they would teach him how to play the violin. His older sisters eventually bought him his own violin, and when he married my mother and moved to Komjat, he brought his violin with him. Every Saturday night after the Sabbath he would take out his violin and we children would sing and dance to his music. When he finished playing, he would return the violin to its cloth case and hang it on the living room wall. When we left home for the ghetto, we left the violin hanging on the wall. If that violin is still in existence, who knows in whose hands it ended up?

My parents renovated the Gelbs' old house, at 470 Masarikova Street in Komjat, the street leading to the village's Jewish cemetery. My parents brought in high-quality lumber and built a big, beautiful house with a porch and a garden, as well as an apartment with a separate entrance for Grandma Chana-Devorah. Later Grandpa Azriel-Tzvi Hershkovits, my father's father, also came to live with us in the boys' room, after his wife passed away.

My father revived the store belonging to our family and turned it into a grocery. In parallel, he hired himself out to plow and harvest and supervise non-Jewish laborers. My father and his brothers owned a threshing machine, which also brought my parents income.

In 1942 our license to operate the grocery was taken away because we were Jews, and its ownership was transferred to non-Jewish neighbors in the village. At that time I couldn't imagine that 70 years later, I would return to see a grocery store in exactly the same location in Komjat, on the property stolen from our family.

As my parents faced the increasing hardships of World War II, my father and his brothers cut down part of the trees that they had inherited from their parents, sold them, and planted new trees in their place.

The home I grew up in was one of giving and helping others. My father volunteered at the Burial Society and was called to assist with every Jewish funeral in the village. He studied *Mishna*[4] as part of the "Mishna Society" in the village, and I remember the many celebrations hosted in our home when chapters of *Mishna* and *Gemara*[5] were completed. I remember our house being open to all, and that we hosted rabbis and traveling preachers who came to visit the village.

Grandma Chana-Devorah, my mother's mother, was a righteous woman and performed many acts of kindness. She was born in Komjat to Bluma and Shmaya Klein, a rabbinical judge.

One stormy winter day during my childhood, my father called me before I left for school in the morning. He pulled

---

4   *Mishna:* The first major written collection of the Jewish oral law, compiled in the 3rd century C.E.

5   *Gemara* (also known as the *Talmud*): A commentary on the *Mishna*. There are two versions of the *Gemara*, one published about 350-450 C.E. and the other about 500 C.E.

a packet of money from his pocket and asked me to go to a certain family in the village. "Knock on the door, go in, say 'Good morning,' put the money on the table, and leave without saying anything. Keep it a secret and don't tell anyone." In the afternoon, when I got home from school, my mother called me, handed me a basket full of food, and whispered to me that I should go to the same family. She said, "Knock on the door, say 'Good afternoon,' put down the basket, and leave, and don't say anything to anyone about it, because it's a secret." I did as my mother had told me. Late that afternoon, Grandma Chana-Devorah called me over, gave me a basket full of food covered with a napkin, and asked me to go to the same family. She said, "Knock on the door, say 'Good evening,' put the basket down, and leave. Don't tell anyone about it, because it's a secret." I said to my grandmother, "It's okay. You don't have to keep the secret from each other. Maybe next time coordinate among yourselves so that I can just go once to bring the money and the two baskets. . ."

Grandma Chana-Devorah took care of a girl in our village named Chavaleh who had lost her father. Chavaleh lived with my grandmother, who raised her with great devotion and eventually married her off when she grew up. I was about 12 when Chavaleh got married, and I remember my grandmother's love for her. After her marriage, Chavaleh lived with her family at the end of our road. She was taken to Auschwitz with us and met her end there, together with her children.

Grandma Chana-Devorah died in 1942 and had the good fortune to be buried in Komjat alongside her parents and husband. Her grave remains there to this day.

The longing to move to the Land of Israel was in the air we breathed in our home. We knew that it was our destiny to move there, but not yet. When the time was right, in a little while. We had two cousins who lived there, and I knew their addresses by heart and often imagined us living there, too.

One Sabbath in 1943 my father came home from the synagogue, flushed with excitement. He called us to look out the window, and we saw that a battalion of hundreds of Jewish soldiers had "settled" in our snow-covered yard. They had been forcibly drafted into the Hungarian army and sent to hard labor. The soldiers had taken shelter under the roof of the wood shed that we used to have in the yard. My father called with excitement, "Children, children! Can you believe that there are Jewish soldiers in our yard? Jewish soldiers! It's like the army we're going to have in the Land of Israel! Soon, in a little while, we'll all move to the Land of Israel."

My father made the blessing over the Sabbath wine for the soldiers and arranged communal prayers for them. We all went out to talk to them, and gradually more Jews from the village arrived to speak with the Jewish soldiers. My parents took our Sabbath dinner and gave it to the soldiers, and our neighbors did as well. That Sabbath we ate nothing more than bread dipped in milk, but we felt tremendous pride to be hosting Jewish soldiers. The soldiers remained in our yard for about four more weeks.

My father's siblings and most of my mother's siblings lived with their families in Komjat or neighboring villages. We saw them frequently, and I heard stories about every one of them. For example, there was the story about Sheyve, my mother's younger sister, who had been a great beauty in her youth. One day a tall, rich Gentile from Komjat came into my grandmother's store and said to her, "If you give me a glass of vodka, I'll tell you a secret."

My grandmother gave him a drink, and he said that even if he were to risk being shot to death, he would have to kiss Sheyve if she passed by him. Frightened, my grandmother ordered a carriage that very evening and sent Sheyve to the village of Bogrovitz. Again they called for David Shmil Avram and asked him to find a good match for Sheyve. This time the matchmaker suggested his nephew. Sheyve was thus married off to Haim Anshel Weiss from the village of Urdo, next to Komjat. Haim Anshel's family was very wealthy. They had endless fields of wheat, tobacco, corn, and potato, and every field was given a special name. A year later Sheyve gave birth to their son, Israel, who was a few months older than me.

On those horror-haunted nights in the quarantine block in Auschwitz, I thought about my family, on both my mother's and my father's sides, who were apparently at that time making their way in trains, as we had done, to Auschwitz. We were on the first transports of Hungarian Jews sent to Auschwitz, and therefore some of us were taken to work and thus kept alive. Rumor had it that in May, 1944, Auschwitz reached its full capacity of Jews, and therefore all the transports arriving after us were sent straight to the gas chambers, since no more workers were needed.

Each morning and evening, when we stood at roll call in

the yard of the quarantine block, I watched the thick, black smoke rising from the crematorium chimney. In those weeks it operated day and night, and I understood that the murdered ones whose bodies were being burnt and ascending to heaven included my aunts and uncles and cousins.

In time I came to learn that I had been right. On June 1, 1944, as well as the day after, a large part of my extended family arrived in Auschwitz and was sent straight to the gas chambers. Almost none of them survived. My mother's younger sister Sheyve, who was then 35, also arrived in Auschwitz then with her husband and their seven children – Israel, Eliezer, David-Melech, Yakov-Hirsch, Bluma, Shalom, and two-year-old Chana-Devora, who was born after my grandmother's death and named for her. The moment they set foot in Auschwitz, their death sentences were sealed.

During those first two weeks in Auschwitz, my soul was torn between mourning the loss of my family and the need to struggle for my own survival.

I Am in the Pit

I am in the pit, and I am screaming.
If I am screaming – I am alive.
If I am alive – how and why am I in the pit?
My family and friends are not in the pit
And they are not alive.
I heard their last cry.
They did not die and were not buried,
Instead, they were poisoned and strangled.
I did not bury my loved ones,
I did not mourn, did not cry,
Did not rend my clothes[6],
Did not sit *shiva*[7] for them,
Did not say *Kaddish*[8] for them.
There is no dead body, no funeral,
I put up no tombstone, because there is no grave.
I carry their memory within me.

---

6   Jews rend their clothing (usually a shirt) upon hearing of the death of a family member.

7   *shiva* (seven [days]): Jews observe a seven-day public mourning period following the death of a close family member. It is known as "sitting *shiva*" because the mourners sit on low seats or on the ground.

8   *Kaddish*: From the root meaning "holy." *Kaddish* is the mourner's prayer that a Jew says daily for the 11 months following the death of a parent, and then annually thereafter on the anniversary of the death.

Fate chose me,
To continue telling the story.
Therefore I eulogize them and tell their story.
Tell the story and speak
Of the terrible destruction
And pass on its events
In pain to future generations.
I ordain the youth
And ask them to continue telling the story,
To remember and never forget,
And never forgive!
Ask of Heaven and wish for
All good things and all blessings to the people of Israel,
To the State of Israel, in the Land of Israel. May it be His will.

SEVENTY YEARS LATER

I was about four years old when I understood that my parents were Holocaust survivors.

A neighborhood boy came up to me and asked, "Your parents are Holocaust survivors, right?" and in fact the question itself contained the answer.

I was still living in the innocent world of childhood, full of joy, playing street games with dozens of neighborhood children until sunset, climbing trees on our street or taking a secret walk out to the edge of the bare hill opposite our house. Yet at the same time another reality was forming in my soul, of a different world, murky and broken, in which the event called "The Holocaust" took place.

As a young girl I was not capable of asking my parents what a "holocaust" was and what happened to them there. My parents and older sisters, Dalia and Dorit, heaped love and attention on me. I was an alert, curious child who loved to ask questions, but in anything connected to the "holocaust" I felt the need to tread carefully, not ask, not investigate, and not cause pain. Subconsciously I understood that whatever my parents had undergone there involved tremendous pain.

Occasionally my mother took me to visit her cousins or

friends from the past. Many times my mother and her relatives would fall on each other's necks, sobbing with pain and longing for something that had been taken from them and was now missing from their world. On rare occasions I would hear my mother cry out or sob in her sleep at night. I knew that everything was somehow connected to what had happened to them, but I was afraid to ask. I did not want to cause pain and anguish.

The village children spoke in whispers about the Holocaust survivors in our neighborhood. They liked to make fun of one of them, an elderly, childless man who lived alone. While the older children hid in the bushes, one of the "brave" boys would ring the old man's doorbell and then run away. Sometimes I would join the younger children in watching the show from our own hideout in the bushes. The neighbor would emerge from his house with raised brows and pursed lips, cursing in Hungarian, and chase us away. We would run out of his yard, howling with laughter. The children said he was crazy, that he had "lost a screw" in the Holocaust. They liked to annoy him and watch his outbursts of rage.

During summer vacation, when the teasing increased in frequency, the old neighbor would open his door with a cup of water in his hand, which he would dump in our direction. Apparently it was already clear to him that we were the ones ringing the bell, even before he opened the door.

Once during summer vacation, when I was five or six, my mother called me over and asked me to stop participating in the pranks that the children were playing on the neighbor. "He is an old man," my mother said quietly. "He has had a hard life. He has been through difficult things. We need to help him and respect him and not bother him." Thus a new insight joined my vague fund of information about the "holocaust" – someone who was there had "a hard life" and went through "difficult things."

I accepted what my mother said and gave her my word. After that I tried to come up with new games in order to keep the neighborhood children away from the old neighbor. If the older boys decided to bother him anyway, I would step aside and convince my friends to play a different game. In my imagination, a hidden alliance was made between that elderly neighbor and my parents, and I treated his hidden, painful past with respect and awe.

Today, more than 40 years later, I hope that the lonely neighbor had other people besides us children ringing his doorbell, people who, unlike us, rang the bell in order to pay him a visit and inquire about his health.

IN THE QUARANTINE BLOCK OF AUSCHWITZ

The two weeks we spent in quarantine were very difficult. We were not used to sleeping crowded together onto one bed with so many others. There was a married woman among us who would constantly complain, saying, "I'm already used to sleeping in my own bed." We understood her.

The dress we wore constantly, without changing or laundering it, looked frightful, full of stains, stinking, and torn. It was the only thing we had on our bodies because we hadn't been given undergarments. Not having found any way to cut my long dress and adapt it to my size, I had to tie up the hem in order not to trip on it.

We didn't have a single thing to our names. No paper to write on, no pencil, no pen, no needle or thread, no comb, no hairpin, no watch, no toothbrush, no toothpaste, no scissors, no ribbon to tie, no cotton, no belt, no salt, no sugar, no oil, no soap, no face cream, no salve for cuts. Nothing.

For two weeks we did nothing, just stood for hours in roll call and went through selections. We stood outside the block from morning to night. Since they didn't take us to the toilets during the day, and knew that we would relieve ourselves standing up, they preferred that we do it outside and not in the clean, well-scrubbed block. Only at night, when it was time to sleep, did they allow us to go inside the block.

I cried incessantly, overwhelmed with grief and pain. I don't remember myself ever smiling or laughing, or finding any consolation. There was no consolation. Everything was done on command: Get up! Go to the toilet! Stand in line! Eat! Go to sleep! Like robots. Like puppets on a string.

Our hunger increased by the hour. In the morning we received a small piece of bread and in the afternoon a bowl of soup. The bowls were like those that, in our home, we placed next to the bed for performing the ritual handwashing on awakening. They were enameled, of different sizes and colors, perhaps stolen from the possessions of people who had arrived at the camp.

The bowl held turbid soup with a few pieces of unpeeled turnip or kohlrabi, together with the greens. All 14 girls who slept together on the board were grouped together, and we received one such bowl for all of us. We were constantly crowded together as a group. We divided up the bowl of soup among ourselves with great consideration. Each one, in her turn, took three sips; if there was a little liquid left in the bowl, we started a new round in which each girl took an additional sip. Consideration for each other came naturally, for we all shared the same fate.

During this period, we were not given supper at all. The nights were very cold, and it is even harder to bear the cold when one is hungry. We slept crowded together, and one wool blanket served all 14 girls on the board, without mattresses or pillows. Nevertheless, I was so exhausted and hungry that I fell asleep as soon as my head touched the board. I was broken by exhaustion and hunger. Every evening I would cry, and fall asleep crying.

The bathrooms were a seven- or eight-minute walk from our block, but prisoners were not allowed to go alone to use them. Therefore, during the night we would use buckets that had been placed in the block. Whoever was lucky enough to get to the bucket when it was still empty could return to the board quickly and go back to sleep. Someone less lucky, however, who reached the buckets when they were full to the brim, was made to drag two sloshing buckets to the toilets, alone in the dark and the cold.

Sometimes the women would joke bitterly about our condition. Someone said one morning, "But I'm used to washing my hands and face in the morning . . ."

One Thursday night someone said, "My Sabbath *cholent*[9] is missing just one thing." Everyone asked, "What?" and she answered, "To get out of here . . ."

Many times we got carried away talking longingly of dishes that reminded us of home. Each one recounted what was cooked and eaten in her family. In fact, we talked about food all the time. "Such a *puliszka* (corn porridge) my mother could make . . ." "Such challahs we would bake for the Sabbath . . ."

Sometimes we sang songs of the Land of Israel, such as a song in Yiddish with the words: "Whale, on the great back of the whale we will travel to the Land of Israel . . ."

---

9   *cholent*: A thick stew made before the Sabbath and left on a low fire over-
     night, in accordance with the laws that forbid cooking on the Sabbath.
     (Cooking or lighting a fire?)

Some of the women took on motherly roles. Someone once said to me, for example, "Please, put this slice of bread in your pocket for the night, because otherwise, what will you eat at night?"

There were always women around us who didn't make it through the day – they would collapse, fall, and give up the ghost. There were pregnant women, who were taken away and never brought back. There was a young woman from our village, Hinda Weissman of the Leibovits family, who had taught me how to sew before we were taken from our homes. She was at the beginning of a pregnancy, and it was not yet visible. Later she was sent to Germany. She gave birth in the camp where she was working, and the child was taken from her and killed. Eventually she married again, started a family, and moved to Israel.

Punishments landed on us constantly from all sides by the blokova and the shtubovas – blows, lashes, punches. During the roll calls, female German soldiers would come and point out certain prisoners, and the blokova and shtubovas would immediately take those women out of line and we would never see them again. The selection was essentially to weed out prisoners who didn't look fit for work. During each selection I felt like we were in a giant sieve. Who would fall through the holes and who would remain? I had a powerful drive to live; I wanted to stay alive.

Many of the girls were fair-skinned, and since we often stood in the sun all day long, their skin would be covered with blisters. They were in danger of dying from infection, but they also faced the risk of being pulled out of line in a selection and sent to the gas chambers, so we tried to hide their blisters. The difficulty was that there was nothing to hide them with. I had a naturally swarthy complexion so I didn't get sunburned; thus, in order to help my friends, I stood in front of them in line during roll call and hid their faces from the sun as much as I could.

A NUMBER TATTOOED ON THE ARM

Two weeks had passed since our arrival in Auschwitz, and it was time to get us out of the quarantine block and into the camp's work routine. After all, for that they had kept us alive. First they brought us to the bath house. This time the water flowed continuously. We came out of the showers, dried off in the air, and were brought to a room where we were given clothing. In another room we were given shoes. The clothes and shoes were from transports of Jews who had arrived at the camp, so every garment was different. I received a brown- and orange-checked blouse with three-quarter sleeves and a winter-weight skirt with a brown and white houndstooth check. The blouse and skirt didn't match, but that was unimportant. I didn't even have time to think about the woman who once owned the garments. Of course they had taken my clothes on the first day, too. At the entrance to each room, shtubovas shoved the clothing into our hands, urging, "Go! Quickly!"

From the showers we returned to the same block. Again we stood for roll call, *zahlappell*, and were counted. At midnight they told us that some of us would be sent to work in Germany and some would be staying here. I didn't make any request because I didn't know what would be better – to stay in Auschwitz, or go to Germany.

They asked us all to hold out our hands, and they passed among us to check them. Those who had quick hands – it was unclear to me exactly what they were checking for or how they decided which hands were quick – were sent to Germany. All the rest stayed. Of the 14 girls who slept with me on the board, eight remained.

Those who went to Germany worked in an armaments factory, and later I heard that they worked under relatively good conditions. Those who stayed in Auschwitz, I among them, were transferred to Block 16 in *Lager* (camp) A, in the part of Auschwitz called Birkenau. Gizi and her shtubovas moved there together with us. Later I learned that Auschwitz had something like 40 sub-camps, of which Birkenau was one. I was a little ant in a giant death factory, who had been granted life temporarily in exchange for my labor. There was a well-known sign reading "*Arbeit Macht Frei*" (Work Sets You Free) placed at the entrance to another part of Auschwitz, today called Auschwitz 1; I didn't see it during my first weeks there, but that was the policy at Auschwitz: If you are capable of working, you are freed from death. For now.

After a day or two we were taken to have numbers tattooed on our arms. That day was particularly hot. First they took us to the showers. As we came out they grabbed us forcefully, one by one, and I was filled with terror of the unknown. They commanded us to arrange ourselves alphabetically by last name. I stood in the group of the letter H.

They told us, "They're giving you a number. It won't hurt."

Thousands of women stood in line, and about 20 at a time had their arms tattooed. In Auschwitz everything was done on a grand scale, by the hundreds, by the thousands, like in a factory.

When my turn came, I sat on the chair before the tattooer, who may have been a nurse or may have been just a prisoner who had been given the task of tattooing. She grabbed my arm and, with a needle dipped in blue dye, scraped into my left fore-arm the number A-7807. The process did not take long, but it hurt. The following day the area was swollen and infected, and it healed only a few days later. The number is tattooed on my forearm to this day. In any other circumstances I would have been shocked that they were carving a number into my body by force, as though I were a cow or a sheep in a herd. But I was in Auschwitz, and two weeks in the place had already caused us to lose our sense of self. Moreover, I assume that I was driven then to focus on surviving, and not waste energy resenting the fact that they had turned me into a number and branded it on my body forever, without my permission.

The day after the tattooing, the shtubovas told us that in the next two weeks, tens of thousands of Jews would be arriving in Auschwitz from Hungary, Yugoslavia, and Holland. And indeed, a few days later they woke us early in the morning and told us that we would be going that day to a good, respectable place of work. Someone whispered, "You won't be hungry, be-cause you will be sorting the parcels that the new arrivals are bringing to Auschwitz. They are bringing nice clothes, money and jewelry, cakes, cookies, and bread. You'll no doubt find food in the pockets and be able to eat it when no one is looking."

During the march to the new workplace, someone said she'd heard that this morning 13,000 girls were going out to work. It became the topic of conversation among us that day. All the girls in our block marched to work sorting the suitcases.

We arrived at a clean room full of parcels and suitcases. They instructed us to put on dark blue dresses with white polka dots. There were dresses with large dots and dresses with small dots. They gave everyone white kerchiefs, and each group wore a different color ribbon on top of the kerchief. My friends from Komjat and I were all given red ribbons to wear on top of our white kerchiefs.

They showed us how to do the sorting. They made us stand next to a very long table, open a suitcase or bag, sort the objects into different groups, and place them into cartons. There was a box for fountain pens, a box for toothbrushes, a box for hairbrushes, etc.

I began opening suitcases. Was there anything that couldn't be found there? People had brought with them dried fruit, anti-lice treatments, salves for cuts. Some were about to give birth and had brought the pads that are placed on an infant's navel after the umbilical cord falls off. Some had brought shrouds. Some had even brought wedding gowns. Some had brought dried bread, specially baked so that it would keep. They had brought *tefillin*[10], prayerbooks, *tallitot*[11], and holy books. Everything that a person could have possibly thought he might need was there.

I saw people's whole lives laid out before my eyes. I fingered those lives, the fear and the despair, the hope and the faith. I held in my hands the lives of people who were almost all no longer among the living.

As we had been told, the bags also held lots of food. They warned us not to eat anything, and German soldiers and Jewish kapos stood over us to make sure we didn't take any objects or eat any of the food. When cakes were discovered in a suitcase, the soldiers took them right away, out of the belief that every Jew had diamonds, and perhaps they were hidden in those cakes.

It did happen once that one of us in fact found a diamond inside a cookie, just at a moment when the German soldier was not looking. The workers immediately shushed each other and covered for each other. Someone advised the woman who had found the diamond to go to the toilet and throw it away. One less Jewish diamond for the Nazi machine. And she did in fact get up and get rid of the diamond. Everyone present was sworn not to talk about it lest she be hung and the rest of us punished.

---

10 *tefillin* (phylacteries): Leather boxes containing scrolls with specific Biblical verses that men strap to their forehead and left arm during the weekday morning prayer service.

11 *tallit* (plural: *tallitot*): A ritual fringed garment worn under a man's clothing. Are you talking about tallit katan (under the clothing) or a regular tallit, which is outside the clothing?

SEVENTY YEARS LATER

"Why does your mother have a number on her arm?" I was asked more than once as a child. From this question I understood, from a young age, that not every mother had numbers on their arms. I didn't dare ask my mother about the number and I tried not to stare at it. Only when my mother turned her head, I would steal a quick glance at it, longing to stroke her arm and erase it with love and compassion. So hard did I try not to look at it openly, afraid to cause her pain, that for years I didn't remember the number.

Sometimes I would tell myself, "This time look at it and say it over and over to yourself. You have to remember it!" But only when I was already an adult did I manage to look at it openly and learn it by heart. A-7807.

In search of more information about my mother as a prisoner in Auschwitz, I contacted the Auschwitz-Birkenau Museum in Poland. Their polite response was, "The number A-7807 was given to a prisoner (name unknown) who was sent to KL from Hungary between the dates 5/15/44 and 6/7/44 and was registered in the camp on June 28, 1944."

It turned out that from the day my mother was registered in the camp (KL is an abbreviation for "camp"), for the whole time she was imprisoned at Auschwitz and until today, her name was erased and was not known. She was a number only. In my response to the museum in Poland, I thanked them politely and added, "My mother's name is Sarah Leibovits, formerly Hershkovits. We would be very grateful if you could please write her name in your lists in the museum, next to her number." I thought to myself, if only I could ask all the sons and daughters of Auschwitz survivors to send the museum their parents' names and numbers, so that they could add a person's name next to each number in their lists. Perhaps that would be a small reparation for the warped history that turned prisoners into nothing but numbers. Every person has a name. Every number has a name behind it.

I have heard stories of second- and third-generation survivors who have their parent's or grandparent's number tattooed on their arms. I have also heard of family members who wear bracelets engraved with the number. For me, the number is engraved on my heart. I will never forget it.

In time, when my mother accompanied Israeli youth delegations to Poland, she asked me to write a short piece, as a second-generation Holocaust survivor, that she would read to the students on the trip. The following story burst forth from me of its own accord. I wrote it when I was 30 years old, and it is seemingly about another girl, 40 years ago, and not about me . . .

Today I know that I wrote it about myself.

She was a little girl, no more than four, when she understood that the bluish number drawn on her mother's delicate, beautiful arm will never come off in the shower, or in the sea.

A little girl with big thoughts, and even though no one ever told her so, she knew that this number was bound up with great pain and sorrow – for who would draw a number on herself that could never come off?

Every chance she got, she would glance at the number, converse with it wordlessly, ask it all the questions. Sometimes, when her mother didn't feel it, she would stroke the arm in the air, touching/not touching the number, as though she wanted to soothe the pain, blur the searing and the fire that it left permanently in her whole body, to forget what her four-year-old brain already knew – without having heard any explanations, without ever having been given any details.

Once, when her mother was cleaning the house before the Passover holiday, the girl glanced over and saw her mother shaking out an old, faded striped gown.

"What's that?" the girl asked in a voice that held wisdom and maturity.

"It's nothing. When you're older I'll explain it to you," the mother hurriedly answered, in a voice of grief and tension.

"Can you tell me anyway what that is?"

But the mother had already folded the garment and stuffed it into the top of the closet, packed inside a paper bag. But the girl could not forget the striped garment. She understood that the garment was tied to the number. Its partner, twin, and constant companion.

One day the girl discovered another object connected to those two. She was looking for something in the drawers next to her mother's bed and found, to her surprise, an old, scraggly clothes brush.

What is an ugly brush doing in her mother's clean, sweet-smelling drawer? The girl didn't know the answer, yet she didn't want to ask, not wanting to cause pain or sorrow, and certainly not tears. She sensed that the brush was also a remnant from somewhere far away, from that nebulous place that made her mother scream at night.

When the girl's father bought her a present of colored markers, ones that no other child she knew had ever had, her mother got angry at him.

"The girl might draw on her hand. She's too little for those markers."

"Why would I draw on my hand?" The girl did not understand.

"Do you promise not to scribble on yourself? Not to draw numbers on your arm?"

And she was always careful and strove to be good and industrious and disciplined – without having heard any explanations, without ever have been given any details.

A little girl, more than 40 years ago.

MEETING MY FATHER, JACOB HERSHKOVITS, IN AUSCHWITZ

Our days passed in suffering, hunger, and exhaustion. Every day we worked from sunrise to sunset, sometimes for 12 hours straight. Many prisoners became ill with typhus, dysentery, and other diseases born of poor hygienic conditions and malnourishment.

On one of my days working at sorting clothing, sometime in the month of June, I went out to the yard with a carton full of fountain pens that had been collected from the parcels. I was charged with bringing the carton to a train car and handing it over to a German soldier who stood there. I was carrying the carton of pens and looking around me. The weather was pleasant, but the smoke rising from the chimney did not let me forget for a moment that I was in Hell on Earth. I thought to myself – I never had a fountain pen. But if I take a pen from the carton and hide it, I'm likely to get caught, and if I get caught I will be beaten to death.

I passed by a double barbed-wire fence. The fence closest to me was electrified, and the one attached to it was a regular fence. On the other side of the double fence passed a security road on which German soldiers rode in their military vehicles, holding guns, and on the other side of that road was another double fence. The fences were arranged such that on the side of the road where the German soldiers rode or walked were regular fences, while on the prisoners' side were electrified fences. Anyone who touched such a fence would be instantly electrocuted to death.

Suddenly I heard someone calling me from beyond the road and the fences:

"Fraulein Hershkovits, Suriko!"

The word "Fraulein" is a respectful term for an unmarried woman, and only polite people used it. I looked around and identified the man. It was Moshe Marmelshtein, our neighbor from Komjat!

I asked him, "Herr Marmelshtein, what are you doing here?"

He answered me, "Your father is here, too!"

I asked him to run and call my father. I stood waiting tensely, overwhelmed with the thought that my father was alive and that I would soon see him.

I heard Marmelshtein call: "Herr Hershkovitz, Reb Yankl, *ayere tochter iz oif die andere zayt vin dem ploit* (your daughter is on the other side of the fence) and I spoke to her!"

I heard my father say in a clear voice, "*Moishe, vus sugste?*")What did you say?)

But I didn't hear Marmelshtein's reply, because at that exact moment a loud siren sounded, and the men from the other side of the fences lined up in rows of five and marched away from there.

Thus I learned that my father was still alive.

I knew that the crematorium was on the other side of those fences. It was hidden among the trees, but we saw great quantities of smoke emerging from the ground.

I brought the carton to the place where I was supposed to turn it in and, sobbing bitterly, walked back to where the girls were sorting. They were frightened and asked me what had happened, thinking that perhaps I had been beaten by a kapo. I told them that I had seen Marmelshtein and heard my father, and that both of them were working on the other side of the fences.

My friends said, "Oh my God, *gevalt*, that's the crematorium there!" And I understood that my father worked in the *sonderkommando*. The word "sonderkommando" means "special unit," and it was the hardest and most terrible work in the Nazis' extermination camps. Its members, who were Jewish prisoners chosen by the Nazis for this work, were forced to remove the Jewish corpses from the gas chambers and burn them in the crematorium. There were several crematorium buildings in Birkenau, and my father worked in one of them.

My father, as I have said, was a Torah scholar, an honest merchant, and a good man. My heart ached to think that such a good-hearted man, full of tenderness and compassion, had to do such strenuous, humiliating work.

I thought that perhaps my father, like me, felt great hope now, having learned that at least I was still alive. From that moment, my father and I began writing notes to each other and tried to find ways to transmit them. We also tried to meet across the fences, even if only for a few moments.

Shoni Solomon, my cousin, was with my father when they were pulled aside in the first selection after we got out of the train. Shoni later told me how my father was chosen to work in the sonderkommando: "On our second day in Auschwitz, Friday morning, German officers came into our block and told us, 'Good morning. You've come to a welcoming, beautiful, good place. Who wants to see his wife today?' They requested that anyone who wanted should step out of the line, and Uncle Jacob stepped forward. I begged him, *Feter* (Uncle), don't go. They'll send you to war!" but Uncle said, 'I am going.' Again I begged, 'Uncle, don't go, they're tricking us,' but his desire to see his wife and perhaps his children was too strong, and he was taken with some other men. Of course they didn't show them their wives, but rather took them to work in the crematorium." During his whole time in Auschwitz, he never saw my father again. Shoni himself survived, immigrated to the Land of Israel, and raised a family.

As I said, my father had been the community leader in our village, the manager of the synagogue, and a volunteer in the burial society. He attended all the funerals of Jews in the village. Even in the dead of winter, when the funeral was held on a rainy or snowy day, he would take his tools out to the cemetery and dig a grave, together with the other burial society members.

Together with my friends, I started to think of ways to meet with my father across the fences. We knew that on Saturday nights the Germans drank wine and got drunk, and that it was hard for them to get up on Sunday mornings, so they would arrive late to work. Accordingly, on Sunday mornings I would go out to deliver the cartons more frequently. The girls agreed to switch with me so I could go out instead of them.

I had not yet managed to meet with my father, but I received notes from him, which he managed to transmit to me via other prisoners or the blokova. We found out that my father was part of a group of nine people from Komjat who were sent to work in the sonderkommando.

One day I went out carrying a carton of shoes, and suddenly, across the fences . . . Father! He wore a blue and gray striped uniform and a cap of the same material. I quickly crouched down in the weeds. My father also crouched down on the other side of the fences and we managed to talk. We made sure no one saw us, for if they had seen us talking to each other we would have been shot immediately.

My father cried, saying, at least 50 times, "*Die mamme lebt nisht mer . . . die kinder ochet nisht.*" (Mother is not alive . . . neither are the children.)

I already knew that my family members were no longer alive, but it pained me greatly to see my father's pain now. I knew that I had to stay alive, if only for his sake.

My father and I managed to meet four times during that period. Mostly we met on Sunday mornings, always through four barbed wire fences, and always for only a few seconds. My father feared that a Nazi soldier would see us and shoot us on the spot.

Once I met my father on his way back from work. I asked my friends to let me stand on the right end of the row, closer to the fence, and the girls made space for me. When we reached the point where I saw my father across the fences, I continued marching in place, while the rows of girls advanced next to me, so that we could speak together for a few seconds.

In the notes that my father sent me, he wrote that he knew that he was not long for this world, since every three or four months they took the sonderkommando workers out to be executed. The Nazis were careful to destroy evidence and to kill everyone who had seen with their own eyes the workings of their extermination machine. In that meeting, he said that he knew his days were numbered. Then, I knew, I would have no one left in the world.

At another meeting I told my father that I was tormented by the fact that I was eating non-kosher food, and my father cried, "Eat everything!"

In one of the notes, my father wrote a sort of will, in pencil on white paper. I saved that note for a long time, but after liberation they took my clothes, with the note inside, and burned them for fear of typhus. I lost the note, but I knew its contents by heart, and it was always with me in my thoughts. About a year after the liberation from Auschwitz I wrote down my father's words, written in Yiddish, as I remembered them:

"To you, my dear daughter Suriko. Promise me, my daughter, to walk, to travel, to the Land of Israel, to Palestine, to marry and raise a family. Build your home in the Holy Land of Israel. There you will be a *Yiddishe Mamme*[12], there you will have a true Jewish family and create a memorial and continuation of our glorious family. Do not seek possessions, fields, and forests. And do not return to Komjat. May you have blessing and success, Tati."

My father sent me three notes in total. In addition, a few times another girl from our group received a note from her father, who also worked in the sonderkommando, and it included greetings from Yankel to Suriko.

---

12   *Yiddishe Mamme*: Jewish mother (in Yiddish).

Alleyway

I had an alleyway,
With no electric lights and no exit.
It was narrow and a bit dark,
And I ran through it barefoot.
It is far away and long gone,
I loved that alleyway very much . . .

I had an alleyway, without glory and without sparkle.
One house stood in it – so strong and solid.
A beloved family lived in it,
We lived in our home in honor and tranquility.
It is far away and long gone.
I miss that alleyway so.

I am in mourning, crying over its loss,
And even more over its destruction.

PAINFUL MEMORIES AND LONGINGS
FOR FAMILY AND HOME

The encounters with my father reminded me each time of our family and our home in Komjat. We lived in the Carpathian Mountains, in a rural area steeped in green, with spectacular views, where many Jews had lived for generations, worked the land, and lived an observant way of life.

Until the end of World War I, the area was part of the Austro-Hungarian Empire. At the end of the war, a new state, Czechoslovakia, was established, and we became part of it. The first president was Tomáš Masaryk, and many streets were named after him, including our street, Masarikova. At the beginning of 1939, when I was 11, the country was split into two – Czechia and Slovakia – and we remained within Czechia. A few months later the Germans invaded Czechia, and the Carpathian region became part of Hungary. Our street was renamed "Horthy Miklos" after the Hungarian ruler of that period. Because of these constant changes, even as a child, I could speak Yiddish, Czech, Hungarian, and a little Russian.

In 1944 the area was liberated by the Soviets and returned to Czechia, but was eventually given over to the Soviet Union. The village is currently known as Veliki Komyati and is part of Ukraine.

Our house was built of wood and covered with plaster inside and out. The ground floor had the large family rooms, the living room and kitchen, and we stored foods such as beans and corn in the attic. The chimney was equipped with a special device for smoking meat. Our house, like other houses in the Carpathian region, did not have electricity, and we used oil lamps for lighting. Our kitchen had an appliance that was then considered modern – a pump that drew water directly from the well to the house.

My father worked in the corn and wheat fields, ran the small grocery store attached to our house, and also, with his brothers, managed the forests that belonged to their father, my Grandpa Azriel-Tzvi Hershkovits. My grandfather died in 1940 and was buried in the village of Bogrovitz. After his death, the forests were not passed on to his sons, since the Germans forbade Jews from inheriting property. My grandfather's property and assets were therefore turned over to the Hungarian government.

I was the oldest child in the family. We were very well brought up. We grew up in a Torah world with values such as helping each other, doing good deeds, and fear of Heaven.

My sister Ruchi (Rachel) was two years younger than me. She had big blue eyes, and she was very smart, hard-working, and quick. We were good friends.

My brother Lazar (Eliezer) was four years younger than me. He also had big blue eyes and blond hair. The boys in our family wore long sidecurls, and Lazar's sidecurls were beautiful and golden. He was very smart, and a diligent student in *cheder*. He was also very quick and knew how to help Mother put the bread in the oven. Lazar would have celebrated his *bar mitzvah*[13] in the month of Cheshvan (October/November) 1944. Before we were taken from our home, we had discussed the fact that immediately after the Shavuot holiday, Lazar would start learning the Torah portion for his *bar mitzvah*, but he never got to do that.

I remember a special story concerning my brother Lazar and me a few years earlier. It was after a week in which rain had fallen non-stop. When we got up on Friday, we heard that the river had flooded the fields. The adults were worried about the crops, but we children were happy to play in the mud. My mother called me and Lazar, gave us a cloth bag that she had sewn herself – which, like everything else in our home, was laundered, fragrant, and ironed – and asked us to go to the field of green beans, whose branches were propped up with sticks, and try to harvest and save as much of the beans as possible.

Lazar and I went out to the fields carrying the white sack, and we wandered along the river to look at the flooding. Suddenly, a few meters away from the river, we saw a giant fish, about a half-meter long, swimming in a puddle, unable to return to the river. It was the kind of fish we called *chuko*, similar to a carp, which was kosher, and we would catch such fish in the river and eat them. But we had never heard of anyone catching such a large fish with his fishing rod. Lazar and I were very happy. Everyone who passed by laughed and rejoiced with us at our find. We took one of the poles holding up a bean plant and tried

_____

13   *bar mitzvah:* A ceremony and celebration marking a boy's thirteenth birthday, when he becomes obligated to fulfill the commandments of Jewish law.

to use it to get the fish into the sack. The sack filled up with mud and dirt, and we were also covered with dirt from head to toe. But after great effort, we managed to get the fish into the sack and drag it home, rejoicing and laughing. When my mother saw us, she wasn't so happy. She felt bad about the sack, whose color had changed to a muddy brown, and wanted us to return the fish to the river. But Grandma Chana-Devorah, hearing the commotion, convinced my mother to keep it. When my father got home, he cleaned the fish, which weighed 10 kilos. My parents set up a large table in the yard and gave out portions of the fish's flesh to all the neighbors. Half the village ate the fish that Sabbath, and the story continued to be told for a long time.

My brother Yosef-Shalom was six years younger than me. He was named Yosef after my father's eldest brother, who was a *Doktor-Rabiner* (a rabbi). This uncle immigrated to the Land of Israel in the 1930s and became a lecturer at the Hebrew University on Mount Scopus in Jerusalem. My brother's second name, Shalom, was after my Grandma Chana-Devorah's brother. Yosef-Shalom was blond, with long beautiful sidecurls and blue eyes. He was a quick, intelligent child, loved by everyone.

My sister Faige was eight years old at the time of her death in Auschwitz. She was a beautiful child with greenish-brown eyes and long brown hair. About a year before we were taken from our home, she and I went for a walk in the fields to see the crops before they were harvested. Faige was a very sharp-witted child. She understood everything and knew everything. She went ahead of me in the field, walking tall and sure of herself. I remember looking at her with love and thinking that she had long, beautiful arms and legs, and, in general, that she was beautiful and sweet. In time, when my first-born daughter Dalia was born, I thought that she was beautiful like Faige. As a child, she also had long beautiful arms and legs.

My baby sister Pessele died in Komjat of whooping cough at age nine months. It happened right after the death of Grandpa Azriel-Tzvi, when my father was still sitting *shiva* for his father. The baby's sudden death was a great tragedy for all of us, and we all cried and mourned her.

My little brother Hershele (Azriel-Tzvi) was born soon after this, and was named after my grandfather. Hershele also had blue eyes and blond hair; he was a beautiful child, smart and very sweet. He was almost three when he was murdered at Auschwitz.

In Komjat I went to a mixed nursery school for Jews and Gentiles. There were about 20 children in our class, and the Hungarian nursery school teacher was called Tukacs-Neini, Mrs. Tukacs. I also attended primary school in Komjat, also in a mixed school for Jews and Gentiles. I remember my excitement before entering first grade, and I remember the pencil case they bought for me, made of brown leather and shaped like a little suitcase. I was so excited that in the summer before I started school, I took my pencil case with me wherever I went. I loved learning and I was a conscientious student.

Every morning I would walk with my little brothers, who attended my school or the adjacent nursery school. My brother Lazar had school until 12:00 and then went with all the Jewish boys to study in *cheder*. I would return home, pick up the lunch that our mother had prepared for him, and bring it to the *cheder*, so that he wouldn't lose any of his study time. Every Thursday evening, Lazar would tell our father what he had learned that week in *cheder*, and my father was very proud of him.

On Monday afternoons, all the Jewish children in the village studied Hebrew with a Jewish teacher, who received a salary from the Czech government. On Sunday mornings we learned Judaism with a *melamed*[14] who was hired by the Jewish residents of the village.

When I was in 9th grade, in September 1943, I began to go to a high school for accounting and business in the neighboring village of Salish. It was very difficult to get accepted to this school, and there were very few Jews there. But I excelled in math and passed the entrance examinations with ease.

I loved my studies, but not even three weeks had passed when, before the Jewish New Year, the principal came into the classrooms and announced, "This Saturday there will be classes and there will be a very important lesson. Anyone who does not come to class on Saturday . . . should not come to school anymore." I cried about it, but neither my parents nor I hesitated for a moment, for it was clear to all of us that one does not desecrate the Sabbath. Thus, with great sorrow, I left my high school studies.

That winter, all Jewish children were expelled from the schools in the region. My parents, together with other parents, hired a private teacher for the boys, who continued to teach them at home. I was sent by my mother to learn sewing with a Jewish girl in the village, Hinda Weissman, from the Leibovits

---

14   *melamed*: An itinerant Jewish teacher. (teacher of Jewish studies?)

family. The sewing skills I acquired with Hinda stayed with me in my sewing work for many years.

My sister Ruchi, who was then 13 1/2, was sent to learn knitting at a knitting salon in the village. There was a room there in which women knitted sweaters, socks, and hats for soldiers at the front. The garments were knitted from angora and sheep's wool that had been spun by hand. Ruchi picked up the arts of spinning and knitting very quickly, and soon she was teaching us knitting at home. We knitted under her direction and earned a bit of money.

Jews made up about a quarter of the village population, and relations between us and our Gentile neighbors were generally good, based on mutual respect. Today not a single Jew is left in the village, but in those days Komjat was considered an important Jewish center. There was a large synagogue in the village, as well as study halls, a *yeshiva*[15], and a cheder. Our village had a ritual slaughterer, a rabbi, a melamed, cantors, adjudicators of Jewish law, and rabbinical judges. One of the rabbinical judges was my great-grandfather, Shmaya Klein.

Until World War II there were very few open expressions of anti-Semitism in Czechia, but the war was hard on everyone, on Gentiles as well as Jews, and there began to be incitement against Jews. This was mostly among young people, as if they thought the war was the Jews' fault. Thus anti-Semitism filtered down to our village as well.

One Sabbath eve in 1942, my father was beaten up as he was returning home from the synagogue. Another time, the

---

15   *yeshiva*: A seminary where men, high school age and up, study Torah.

Hungarian army entered the village on Friday, and the soldiers confiscated the challahs that we had baked. Some feared that the soldiers would confiscate the Sabbath candlesticks that had been passed down through the generations, so they hid them and lit Sabbath candles that had been stuck into potatoes.

Before Yom Kippur of 1943, we heard that the Gentiles were planning to steal the chickens that we had prepared for the ritual of *kapparot*.[16] We had a guard dog in our yard, and we hoped that he would keep away the criminals, but a few Gentiles threw the dog some meat laced with needles, causing the dog's death, and stole the chickens during the night.

Around the holiday of Purim, in March 1944, we were ordered to wear yellow patches identifying us as Jews. At this stage, anti-Semitism in our village had increased, and was now out in the open. The Germans entered the village and circled it in their military vehicles. The Gentile villagers tried to curry favor with the conquerors and welcomed the Germans with a ceremony in which all the children sang, but the Germans were not impressed with the ceremony and left just as it was getting underway. They gave the village leadership the task of organizing our expulsion from our homes, and those leaders fulfilled their assignment faithfully.

Every few days, new signs would appear on the walls of the town hall with the latest decrees. For example, it was forbidden to sell milk to Jews; all Jews had to turn in their horses; and Jews

---

16   *kapparot*: A Jewish ritual before Yom Kippur (the Day of Atonement), traditionally involving slaughtering a chicken and distributing the meat to the poor.

could leave their houses only between 10:00 in the morning and 3:00 in the afternoon.

Due to ongoing, intentional bureaucratic delays, some Jews in the area had not been given official Czech or Hungarian citizenship, even though most of us had lived in the Carpathian Mountains for five or seven generations. And lo and behold, a few days before Passover, a list was hung on the wall of the town hall, bearing the names of village Jews who lacked citizenship and would therefore be required to leave the village soon. We were in shock, but thought that perhaps it was a bureaucratic error that could be taken care of.

Another decree stated that Jews were forbidden to bake *matza*,[17] and anyone who violated the law would be punished. But how could one have Passover without *matza*? We decided to bake *matza* secretly. A few days before Passover – risking our lives – we assembled at midnight in one of the houses and baked *matza* for several families. My sister Ruchi and I kneaded the dough, my father supervised and checked the time according to Jewish law[18], and the *matzas* were put in the oven and baked.

On Passover eve of that last year in our home, my mother sent my brother Lazar and me to the ritual slaughterer of the village with a few of our chickens so that we could cook them for the holiday. On our way back home, a young Gentile neighbor came up to us, grabbed the basket of chickens out of our hands,

---

17   *matza*: An unleavened bread of flour and water eaten during the seven days of the Passover holiday, when leaven is forbidden.

18   By Jewish law, *matza* must be baked within 18 minutes from the moment the water is mixed with the flour; otherwise it is considered to be leavened and therefore forbidden to be eaten during Passover.

threw it into a ditch by the side of the road, and threatened us. We returned home terrified and sobbing.

My mother said, "I'll go talk to the neighbor and tell her to give her son a talking-to."

We walked with my mother to the neighbor, and my mother spoke to her politely. The neighbor scolded her son and told him that he had misbehaved. The son answered his mother, "I'll tell Hitler that you don't support him . . ."

During the week of Passover, new signs appeared on the walls of the town hall, announcing that on the day after Passover, all the Jews in the village would be removed from their homes. To where – we didn't know. There were a few young Jews who ran away from their homes and hid in the forest or with Gentile neighbors, but it never occurred to me to do such a thing. Even looking back, I know that I would not have left my parents alone to handle my younger siblings. Moreover, the general opinion was that there was no point in running away, that anyone who ran away would lose out, while anyone who was law-abiding and didn't make waves would be better off.

On Saturday night, after the Passover holiday was over, my mother sifted flour to bake bread for the way. Because of the holiday, we had no yeast in the house, so my mother baked a sort of pita bread.

Because we were religious Jews and followed the commandments strictly, we had not done any laundry during the seven days of Passover. Thus on that Saturday night we had piles of dirty laundry waiting to be washed. We could barely find a clean undershirt and shirt for each child. We packed clothes, coats, blankets, a few dishes, and a little food, such as beans and potatoes. Since we didn't have enough suitcases, we tied up our belongings in pillow cases and blanket covers. My mother prepared a parcel with Sabbath clothes for my father and herself, as well as embroidered bed linens and embroidered and crocheted tablecloths. She hid the parcel in a pit in the cowshed and covered it with straw.

On Sunday morning, the appointed village officials began to take the Jews from their homes. They started with the houses on one side of the Jewish cemetery, and they reached us, on the other side of the Jewish cemetery, on Monday morning.

There was a knock on the door. Grim-looking men stood in the doorway, uttering the command, "Get out!"

My mother, sobbing, went outside with the other children, and I remained the last one in the house. I looked around for the last time, locked the door, and handed the key to one of the men, a Gentile neighbor, who had been my teacher at school. He pulled out some tape from his pocket, stuck a note on the key, and said to me in Russian and German, "I am very sorry that I have to take you out of your home, but that is the order. I am not guilty. I am just following orders."

They led us on foot to the synagogue in the center of the village, where all the Jews of Komjat had congregated – hundreds of men, women, and children. We waited there for two days, sleeping crowded together on the ground. On the third day, Gentiles loaded us and our possessions onto carts and brought us to the neighboring village of Orshava. They led us to empty houses from which Jews had been taken a few days earlier, and we stayed in those houses for four days.

While we were staying in Orshava, my father walked back to Komjat and entered our house by the back door, taking care that the neighbors wouldn't see him. He saw the dough remaining in the bowl, which we had not had time to bake. The dough had flowed over the sides and dried out. My father collected various items that he thought we might need and returned to us.

A week after we had left our home, they took us in carts to the Orshava train station. There they loaded us onto freight cars and transported us to the city of Munkács.

Munkács was a large city about 40 kilometers from our village of Komjat. The Jewish residents of the city ran various Zionist activities, and there was a Hebrew gymnasium (secondary school) thought to be one of the most important in Eastern Europe, and a source of pride for area residents. When we got to the city, we were brought to a brick and tile factory, formerly belonging to a Jew by the name of Shayevitz. It had been expropriated and turned into a ghetto for 15,000 Jews from neighboring villages. The Jews of Munkács itself were moved to a ghetto that had been set up within the city.

German SS men stood at the entrance to the ghetto, hitting and pushing us and announcing that we could only bring into the ghetto what we could carry on our bodies. It was pouring rain, and we stood at the ghetto entrance for a long time, drenched and shivering with cold. All our possessions, clothing, and blankets got wet. At the entrance, they announced that anyone who had silver, gold, or jewelry had to give it to the German soldiers. To intimidate us, they pulled three young men out of the line, showed us that they had not turned in their silver and gold, and announced that they would therefore be hung. My mother immediately pulled out our jewelry and silver and turned it over to the soldiers.

At the entrance to the ghetto, they separated my father from us by force. He returned to us later without sidecurls or beard, sobbing bitterly. As a girl, the sight of my father shorn of his sidecurls and beard, sobbing, was catastrophic.

My father's uncle, who had formerly lived in the Ukraine, arrived at the ghetto together with us. Two years earlier, the uncle and his family had been taken to a forest in the Ukraine. When he stepped aside to relieve himself, he suddenly heard screams and shots. When he returned, he found his family and all the members of his village left dead in a pit. He ran away and hid, and eventually came to us in Komjat on foot. At that time, when he told us his story, we thought that such things happened only to Ukrainian Jews, but now we had also been expelled from our home. My uncle's beard was also shaved off, and he returned together with my father, sobbing and looking utterly shattered. I said to him, "*Feter*, I'll help you." He cried and said, "Kill me now, right here. I don't want to be in this place."

The brick factory had been in operation for many years, and it was surrounded by giant pits from which red earth was excavated to make tiles. The rains of that winter filled the pits with water. The Germans had removed the ovens and machines from the factory and brought us, thousands of Jews, into the empty factory building. We spent four nightmarish weeks in that place, which my father called "The Gateway to Hell."

The water in the pits served us for washing and doing

laundry, but because there were not enough public bathrooms for everyone, many had to relieve themselves in the water as well. Very quickly the water became contaminated and crawling with lice. Before, when we lived at home, we knew how to protect ourselves from lice, but as soon as we arrived at the Munkács Ghetto, the lice took over everything.

To deal with the lice, they instructed everyone to come to a certain spot in the ghetto to have their hair cut and beards shaved. My mother said that she was not willing to let them cut mine or my sisters' hair. Anyway, our hair was short at that time. My little brother Hersheleh, who was not yet three, was taken with the other children to have his hair cut. All his blond hair was shorn off.

When he came back, he asked tearfully, "Why did they shave off my sidecurls?" For weeks, while we were still at home, we had been preparing him for his *chalakah*[19] ceremony, and we told him that soon he would have sidecurls like his big brothers. And suddenly – everything was turned upside down, even in his small world.

Throughout that spring, rain fell incessantly, as though even the forces of nature had gone crazy. Every day we put a pot outside so it would fill with rainwater for drinking. One of us stayed next to the pot to guard it, lest it be stolen. There were always people who would come and beg, "*A bissele vasser* (a little water) . . .", not having even a pot to put out in the rain.

Hunger in the ghetto was unbearable. Gentiles outside the

_____

19   *chalakah*: A Jewish ceremony in which a three-year-old boy has his hair cut for the first time.

ghetto would sometimes attack the wagon bringing us bread, and no bread would be given out that day. Whenever we did manage to get hold of some bread, every crumb would disappear in the space of a minute. There was a woman with two small children, and we would make sure to give her, or the old woman who had no one to look after her, a few slices of our bread. My mother once went out to the food distribution point and managed to come back with two loaves of bread, but within five minutes not a crumb was left. The children crawled on the floor and licked up the crumbs.

One day my mother asked me to entertain my little brother Hersheleh, because the boy was crying from hunger all the time. I sat down with him on the steps of the ghetto and told him a story. Suddenly he said, "Suriko, maybe you want to give me *a berekele broit*" (a crumb of bread)? My heart went out to him, and I burst out crying. To my great sorrow, I couldn't give him any bread.

A week after that incident we arrived at Auschwitz, and on that day my mother and five siblings were murdered. Now I was alone in Auschwitz-Birkenau, far from my father, who worked at a terrible, horrific job, the hardest job in Auschwitz. I knew that as a worker in the sonderkommando his fate was sealed, and that he would soon be taken out to be killed.

My Dear, Good Parents

I haven't been alone for many months,
Everywhere just women and more women.
In one bed – fourteen women.
A towering chimney of red bricks,
Threatening in their very essence.
Striped clothing,
An electrified barbed-wire fence with searchlights,
A dark avenue and a few trees.
The giant crematorium and some huts.
There – our honored men work.
Among them my father, my teacher, and other Jews.
I saw them humiliated, trembling, puffy-eyed,
Crying without tears, keeping silent and biting their lips.
Their work is cursed, contemptible.
Only Satan could have dreamed it up.
Burning the corpses after the poisoning,
Turning them into anonymous ash and dust.
My father said to me: "My daughter, you are the only one
Of the whole good, glorious family.
You stay alive."
Such simple words.
"On the foundation of this great destruction,
You must go on and build a monument to the family,

Our glorious, good family."
Yes, my father, yes, my mother, my dear, good parents,
The lofty and the righteous,
I have fulfilled your last wish.
I have raised a family in the Holy Land of Israel.
I have a husband, children, grandchildren,
great-grandchildren.
There, in the World to Come, you must know everything
already.

SEVENTY YEARS LATER

I never had a grandmother or grandfather.

There were no elderly people in my immediate surroundings. I never knew the love or caress of someone who loves you with a grandparent's love, who accepts you as you are, with a basket full of treats, with no conditions and no need to discipline you or fit you into a framework.

In my childhood we were a very small family, a family of Holocaust survivors. I had two sisters, Dalia and Dorit; one uncle, Moshe, of blessed memory, my father's brother, who was saved from Auschwitz, ran away and was detained in a prison camp; his wife, Bruria, of blessed memory, also a Holocaust survivor; and two cousins, Tamar and Revital. That was the extent of our immediate family. My parents stayed in close touch with their cousins, mostly Holocaust survivors as well, but saw them mainly at family celebrations.

When I was seven, my eldest niece, Irit, was born. At once I saw a grandparent's love for the first time. I saw that my parents related to their new granddaughter in a very different way from how they treated me, and I longed even more for grandparents' presence in my life.

I approached my mother. "We'll make a deal," I said to her.

"I really want a grandmother, and since I don't have any grandmothers, you'll be my mother and my grandmother." My mother laughingly agreed, and my request became a family joke.

Time did not heal my longing for a grandmother and grandfather, for lots of aunts and uncles and a crowd of cousins. Eventually my desire was fulfilled, and our family grew and grew.

When I traveled with my mother and the Israeli youth delegation to Poland in 2014, I had two peak experiences. One was when we sang *"Hatikvah"*[20] at Auschwitz. I held my mother's hand, and for both of us it was an exciting moment of the victory of light over darkness.

The other powerful experience was at the Auschwitz-Birkenau block when my mother met with several youth delegations and told them about her life as a teenager in Auschwitz. The young people hung onto every word, and many wiped away tears. When she finished speaking, I stood at her side, and together we read out the list of her children, grandchildren, and great-grandchildren, too many to count, including her great-granddaughter Noga who had been born that very morning. That was my mother's revenge on the Nazis – to stand before young Israelis in the block in Auschwitz-Birkenau and read out the names of her many descendants.

---

20   *Hatikvah*: The Israeli national anthem. The title means "The Hope."

DAILY LIFE IN AUSCHWITZ

For us, life in Auschwitz passed without a clock. We had no way to keep track of time. We didn't see the stars or the moon, perhaps because many times the skies were cloudy, or perhaps because we were too weary to notice them.

They woke us up very early in the morning, when it was still cold and dark outside. With no compromises or yielding, they woke us with shouts, "Hurry, hurry! Get down and go outside!" Sometimes the blokova held a bell that she used to wake us. Of course we didn't change clothes, but continued wearing the same dresses we had slept in. The mornings were frigid; we shivered with cold and our teeth chattered. Even after we had gotten out of bed, the blokova continued shouting, and everyone hurried outside. Often girls stumbled and fell on each other.

The yard was paved with tiles. We stood for the *zahlappel*, the roll call, in rows of five, and the shtubovas passed among us and counted us. The shorter girls stood in front and the taller girls behind them. Every once in a while a German soldier would come and receive a briefing.

At one of the roll calls they suspected someone of being pregnant and they pulled her out of line. If someone had a bad cold – they took her out. If someone had obvious sores – they took her out. If someone looked sick or weak – they took her out. All those taken out of the line disappeared and we never saw them again.

Hinda Weissman from Komjat had an elderly mother and a younger sister, Ruchi, who was my friend. Well before this, when we were still in our homes, Ruchi had begun to suffer from a hump on her back, and she was taken for treatment. At one of the roll calls in Auschwitz they noticed Ruchi's hunchback and took her out of the line. Her mother began to scream and cry, and they took her out, too. Neither ever returned to us. We were sure they were sent to their death, but in time I learned that they were taken for medical experiments. I saw them later on in Auschwitz, but they didn't survive the war.

While we lived in Block 16 we had a regular group of five, and we almost always stood in the same formation. First was Sheyvi Avram, who was 25 and unmarried. Second was her cousin Yidis Avram, who was 12, but looked older than that. Because of her tender age, and because she had lost her father while still in Komjat, we all watched over her. I was the third. The fourth was Malka Deutsch, and the fifth was her sister, Yidis Deutsch.

After morning roll call, each quintet of girls was given the bowl of tea, a dark liquid with no sugar. That was "breakfast" in the camp.

Then we were taken in groups of 100 to use the toilets. From there we were sent to our job sorting clothing. It was summertime, the days were long, and we worked long hours, until dark. On Sundays we worked until noon, and then we were brought back to the block, where we waited idly for the evening. Sometimes they commanded us to stand in the yard and other times they commanded us to lie on the boards.

We were constantly hungry. During our workday sorting clothing, they didn't give us lunch, taking into account that we were occasionally sneaking into our mouths things we found in the parcels. But we could only take food from the parcels when the kapos weren't looking.

Sometimes we would find dried rolls or cookies in the parcels we were unpacking. The girls would tell a joke to distract the kapo who was supervising us, and while she was laughing we would sneak the food into our mouths. If the kapo turned her head back before we had time to swallow, we would get fierce blows.

Sometimes on the way, in the dirt, we would find a vegetable root. If we managed to bend down and pick it without the kapo seeing us, we could suck on it just as it was, unwashed and unpeeled.

When we returned to the block in the evening, there was another roll call where we were counted. They counted us meticulously morning and evening to make sure that no one had escaped, as though it were possible to escape from a place surrounded by electrified fences, where we were watched 24 hours a day. Sometimes we received our "supper" soup outside, during the roll call, and then a bowl was given to each row of five girls. Other times they gave out the soup in our beds, and then the same bowl had to feed the 14 girls on the board. The bowl held bean soup with oats and barley or potatoes in their skins. The soup was watery and thin, sometimes dirty and foul-smelling, and the few sips each of us got were never enough to satisfy our hunger. In the evening, every prisoner received a portion of bread that represented an eighth or a tenth of a loaf. Some girls saved part or all of the bread for the morning, but I preferred to eat it immediately, for fear that someone would steal it while I was sleeping. Sometimes they would give out a cube of margarine together with the bread. Once in a while, on Sundays, they would give out sausage. Everyone ate the sausage even though it was not kosher, because the circumstances demanded eating in order to survive.

In general, the food was paltry and insufficient. We talked about food all the time. Women would remember longingly, "Stuffed cabbage. . . *Nokedli* (dumplings made of dough) . . ." We would all sob, "How could I not have finished the food on my plate when I was at my table at home?"

Most of the time we experienced unbearable hunger, which was a torment in itself. Much later, I discussed with my husband Shalom the meaning of the expression "the shame of hunger."[21] He said, "The shame is what the hunger causes human beings to do." And indeed, more than once in Auschwitz I saw how hunger brought people to shame. Many times I saw women hitting each other and grabbing from each other a quarter-slice of bread. I was not an aggressive girl and never grabbed bread from anyone. Neither did anyone take bread from me, since I never had any extra bread to wave around, as certain girls were wont to do.

The block, like the rest of the camp, was scrubbed clean at

---

21 An expression in Hebrew, based on Ezekiel 30, which means "extreme hunger" but is literally translated "the shame of hunger."

all times. I don't know who cleaned it, perhaps the shtubovas, or other prisoners. But every evening when we came back from sorting clothes, we entered a clean, tidy block, and were ordered to maintain its cleanliness. Anyone who unintentionally soiled it caught blows from the blokova or the shtubovas. In the morning we had to cover the board with the blanket that the 14 of us had huddled under together during the night. Usually the last one to leave the board had the job of spreading out the blanket.

In the middle of the block was a heater that was supposed to burn during the winter to warm us, but I never saw it lit. If one of us sat on the stone barrier around the heater and swung her legs, she would be hit by the blokova. Most of the time we were not allowed to sit around the heater at all, and it remained new and sparkling clean.

There was no water faucet in the block, and we were forbidden to drink from the water in the bathrooms, which contained soda or cleaning agents. In general, we were given very little water to drink. On the way to work, if we saw a puddle of standing rainwater, and got the chance, we would run and scoop up the water with our hands to drink it.

Sometimes we would get drinking water in a special way. On one bed in Block 16 there were several non-Jewish Polish girls, political prisoners who were incarcerated because they were suspected of being Communists. They were given better conditions than the Jewish prisoners, and they would help the shtubovas peel potatoes for the evening soup. My friend Sheyvi Avram was skilled at peeling potatoes and would help them. They would bring a pot of water to wash the potatoes before cooking them. Sheyvi would use a cup to steal a little of this water, in which the potatoes had been washed, for her young cousin Yidis and for me, and we drank that water eagerly.

The block had electric lighting, but we couldn't turn it on or off; only the blokova did that.

One of our biggest fears in Auschwitz was getting our period. Anyone who got her period was taken away and never returned. Later I learned that such women were sent for medical experiments. Fortunately, I didn't get my period even once during my stay in Auschwitz. They told us that the Nazis put bromine in the food or the water to stop our periods and also to calm us, lest we try to kill each other, rebel, or escape.

At night I was so exhausted that I would fall asleep quickly and easily. I would even fall asleep standing up at the zahlappel. I almost never dreamed, apparently from exhaustion. Sometimes at night I heard women next to me sobbing or screaming in their sleep. Once someone screamed, "He's killing me. . ." but no one will ever know what she was dreaming about. Sometimes women would call out family members' names in their sleep, "Moishele, *kim* (come)." Once someone shouted, "*A bissele teh. . .*" but there was no one to give her a bit of tea.

There were instances when food was stolen, but I never told on anyone, not wanting to get hit by the person who had done the stealing. Once my friend Ruchi put her shoes under her head, and while she was sleeping someone removed them. She felt the movement, woke up, and began shouting that someone had stolen her shoes, but her cries were in vain; the one who had stolen them pretended to be asleep. There was a box at the entrance to the block with wooden clogs, and in the morning

Ruchi was forced to take a pair of clogs to wear. It was hard to walk in clogs, and anyone wearing them on a wet floor or on snow was likely to slip.

We were all weak and hungry, and therefore we didn't try to rebel or talk back. The older women among us tried to ingratiate themselves with the kapos in order to obtain certain things, but I kept quiet and never tried to flatter anyone.

Sometimes we would get up in the morning and discover that someone had died during the night. Two prisoners would come in, throw the corpse on a wooden wagon, and cart it away. In such situations, I tried to turn my head and not look. To my great sorrow, it was not a rare sight, and not one of us said "*Baruch Dayan Ha'emet*" (Blessed Is the True Judge)[23]." Death in Auschwitz was our daily routine.

Even then we had already heard the rumor that medical experiments were being performed on human subjects in Auschwitz. Sometimes there were rumors about twins who managed to send a note saying that blood samples were being taken from them. The young and innocent among us did not understand what they needed samples of their blood for, but Haychu Gelb, who at 44 was the oldest of the group of women from Komjat, explained to us the little that she herself scarcely understood then. The name Josef Mengele, the German doctor who directed the horrifying experiments, was known to us already in Auschwitz, and I even saw him a few times from a distance. He was always surrounded by officers, bloated with honor and self-importance.

Every once in a while they took us to the shower in a large

group. After the shower, they shoved clean dresses in our hands, blue with white dots, which we wore day and night, until the next shower. I missed normal human clothes, my clothes, clothes that regular people changed every day.

I remembered the clothes I was wearing when I arrived at Auschwitz. That day, over my shirts, I wore a green sweater that I had knitted myself, when my sister Ruchi taught us to knit. I had chosen a pattern that I had seen and liked, with pockets, buttons, and a special design on the front. To me, the sweater was beautiful. It got left behind on the shelf where I placed it on my first day in the camp. One day in Auschwitz I saw a kapo walking around wearing my green sweater! My sweater, that I had knit with my own hands according to a pattern that I loved! Unable to say a word to her, I just bit my lip until it began to bleed.

We lived in an atmosphere of despair, alongside a certain measure of hope. I believe that every prisoner in such a place chooses her own emotional atmosphere. Many times I saw people in despair, who threw themselves on the electrified fence and committed suicide. At first I was in shock, and even after I had already gotten used to such sights, I regretted their deaths. I thought to myself – No, I won't do anything like that! I will hang on and survive this hell!

Two months after I arrived in Auschwitz, it was my 16th birthday, on July 16, 1944. On the Jewish calendar it came out on a Sabbath on which one blessed the new moon[22] of the month of

---

22   The Jewish calendar is based on lunar months, so the first of each month is the day of the new moon.

Tamuz. We counted days by the secular (Gregorian) calendar, but for figuring out on which Sabbath to bless the new month, we also counted by the Jewish calendar. There were learned girls among us who counted the months and knew when the eve of the new month fell. Thus I knew on which day my birthday fell, but in those years no one made a fuss about birthdays anyway.

Four years earlier, when I turned 12, I got up in the morning and told my mother, "Today is my birthday!" My mother answered me then, "Wonderful, now you can check the cabbage[23] yourself." Likewise on my 16th birthday, I didn't make a big deal out of it. I cried a little. I asked my friends, "I was born for this? For this Auschwitz?" I was my parents' firstborn, after three years of trying to have a child, and for them my arrival was like the coming of the Messiah. And now, on this sad birthday, my mother and my six siblings were no longer among the living.

The others didn't mention birthdays or wedding anniversaries either. If someone said, "Today is my birthday," she would just cry to herself. In Auschwitz, tears were the only way to mark events from our former lives.

---

23 When a Jewish girl turns 12, she becomes obligated to fulfill the commandments of Jewish law. Checking vegetables for insects was a task given only to those old enough to be obligated to the commandments.

THE STRANGE PACKAGE MY FATHER SENT

The fast of *Tisha b'Av*[24] fell on a Sunday in the last week of July. On the Sabbath we worked sorting clothes. We all knew that in the evening, before the Sabbath went out, we would need to eat in preparation for the fast. But things didn't work out as planned. When we were taken back to Block 16 on Saturday evening, they didn't bring us directly into the block, but rather made us stand outside. I dozed off standing up. I don't know how long they kept us outside, but it was already late. We couldn't go to the toilet, and we couldn't sit, only stand. I felt as though roots would soon grow out of my feet and take hold in the soil.

While we were standing and waiting there – without even knowing what for – the blokova came out, approached us, the nine girls from Komjat who had fathers or brothers working in the crematorium, and told us that a package had come for us. One of us took the package aside and we all crowded around her. She opened the package and took out a note in my father's handwriting. He had written, "We are sending you a package and we beg you to make use of it."

---

24   *Tisha b'Av*: The ninth day of the Jewish month of Av, a fast day in mourning for the destruction of the Temple in Jerusalem.

We carefully opened the package and saw a lipstick, face powder, and cream.

A few of the girls said to me, "What's this? Is your father insane?"

I also thought that perhaps the work at the crematorium had made my father go crazy. I had never had face cream, face powder, or lipstick. My mother hadn't worn makeup either. It was generally not accepted in our community.

Haychu Gelb, who was older than the rest of us, had a different perspective. She was a relative of our family from Komjat (her husband Shlomo was my Grandpa Eliezer's cousin). Haychu knew my parents well. She said, "Girls, if Reb Yankl writes something like that – there's a good reason to put on makeup. Come here and I'll make you up."

She took out the makeup and did all our faces. Our pale, emaciated cheeks took on a bit of color, and the dark circles under our eyes faded slightly. On the outside we looked refreshed and more full of life, but what we felt inside could not be colored with any paint.

Suddenly a group of harsh-faced, haughty German soldiers and officers came to conduct a tzahlappel, a roll call. From each row of five girls, they began taking the first one out. Then they scrambled us up, as though we were a deck of cards, and again commanded us to line up in rows of five. This time they changed the rules of the game and took out the first three girls of each group of five. Again they scrambled us up and again took out some of us. Everyone who had been taken out of the line was pulled aside. The Auschwitz camp was crowded in those days, and rumors spread that some of the people were being sent to Germany.

That night all the blocks in the camp were thinned out. The goal was to leave only a quarter of us in Auschwitz. I don't know whether the makeup on our faces helped us stay there. In general, we didn't know what was better, to go or to stay. All we wanted was to survive and stay alive.

At one point they pulled me out of the line. I didn't know whether I was a rejected card in the deck, or one that had been chosen. Haychu Gelb was also taken aside and placed next to me. Her daughter Ribcho remained with the other girls. Both wept bitterly, for they wanted to stay together. They didn't care whether it was better to go or better to stay; the main thing was to be together.

They signaled to me and begged silently, "Let's switch." At a moment when the soldiers weren't looking at me, I switched with Ribcho; she left the line and ran to stand by her mother while I ran to the line and stood in her place. Later I heard that both of them were taken to Germany, worked in a factory there under good conditions, were released, and survived. I remained in Auschwitz.

We stood in the roll call all that night. In the morning everyone who was being sent to work in Germany was loaded on the train. I assume that during that selection, as in every other one, they also took out girls who looked sick and weak, to be sent to the gas chambers.

The next day, on Tisha b'Av, we weren't sent to work sorting parcels, but they left us to sleep outside, on the ground. To our sorrow, we couldn't fast. We had no dishes in which to store the drop of soup we were given at lunchtime so that we could eat it after the fast. We told each other, "When we're back home we'll fast." Anyway, we barely ate even when we were given a meal.

The following day we were already back to our regular work sorting clothes. In the following weeks, the crematoria were working day and night. Auschwitz in those weeks was a diabolical factory of death. Along with the transports from Hungary that arrived, transports also came from Holland, Italy, France, Belgium, Greece, Czechoslovakia, Poland, and Germany. At the end of August the transports slacked off, and rumor had it that soon there would be no one left to transport.

We knew that if the transports ended, the work of sorting the parcels would also end, and we feared our fate. The motto of Auschwitz was "Work Sets You Free," and anyone who didn't have work was no longer useful to the Nazi machine. We didn't want to be useful to any Nazi machine; we just wanted to stay alive, to survive.

One day in August we returned from work sorting clothes and heard that they were about to send all of us to Germany. The Russian front was approaching, and there were rumors that the Russians had already reached the far side of the Vistula River. In the notes we received during this period from our nine fathers and brothers who worked in the sonderkommando, we heard that they were trying to figure out how to get us transferred to another workplace, out of fear that there would soon be a big selection, in which some of us would be sent to Germany and the rest to the gas chambers.

In one of the notes, written in my father's handwriting, he proposed that we ask to be transferred to work in a munitions factory, where there was a work manager from Munkács whom he knew well. He wrote that the manager, named Halperin, would help us learn the job.

A few days after *Rosh Hashanah* (Jewish New Year), they took us to the showers. There were doctors standing there, who examined us naked and carried out a selection. We walked in front of them, one after the other, and they glanced at each of us briefly and signaled with their hands, left, right, or straight ahead. Whoever was told to walk straight ahead – knew that she was staying alive. For the moment. Whoever was sent to the sides knew that this was her last day.

When it was Sheyvi Avram's turn, they sent her to the left, to death. The rest of the girls in our group from Komjat were saved in this selection, but we all cried because they had taken Sheyvi.

While we were showering, they pushed the thousands of girls who had not passed the selection into a storeroom, where they would wait their turn to enter the gas chambers. When we finished our showers, we got dressed, went outside, and lined up in rows of five. We cried, dry-eyed, for Sheyvi.

Suddenly we saw her. She had climbed up on the roof of the tall storage shed where the girls were imprisoned. She called to us: "I'm jumping from here, come what may!"

Standing below, we clustered together and prepared to catch her. She jumped into our arms. Someone gave her a long shirt, and she took her place with us in the row and went back to being one of us. She eventually survived Auschwitz, went to the United States, and raised a family there.

Every morning on our way to work and every evening on the way back we had to sing, on command. The song was always the same, in German, and was apparently an abbreviated version of a German folk song:

IN MEINER HEIMAT
DORT BLÜHEN DIE ROSEN
IN MEINER HEIMAT
DORT BLÜHT DAS GLUCK
ICH MÖCHTE SO GERNE
MIT MEINER MUTTER NACH HAUSE
ICH MÖCHTE SO GERNE
IN MEINER HEIMAT ZURUCK

Its words in English (loosely translated): "In my home, there the roses bloom, in my home, there my good fortune blooms. How I long to be there with my mother, how I long to be home again." We sang that song with great pain, biting our lips, and with wounded hearts. We felt the intense cruelty of the kapo, or those above her, in forcing us to sing it.

As the transports grew fewer, the parcels needing sorting also grew fewer, and another selection was held, after which a significant portion of the girls from our block were sent to Germany. Sheyvi Avram, Yeidis Avram, Malka Deutsch, and Yeidis Deutsch were sent there, and I was the only one left of the five girls who had regularly stood in a row, shared a bed, and gone everywhere together. Later I heard that the train in which they were traveling never made it to its destination. Rumor had it that the partisans had apparently destroyed the railroad tracks. The girls were returned to Auschwitz, although I didn't see them again.

For two weeks they had us carrying boulders. We had to load

wheelbarrows with four or five large boulders and bring them to the Vistula River. Several girls together could barely lift the wheelbarrows and drag them to the river.

For a very short period we also worked in agriculture. We were taken to sow fields belonging to Polish peasants living near Auschwitz, and there was a rumor that the director of the camp earned money from it.

Autumn was approaching, the days were getting shorter, and part of the work was done in the dark. Even when we returned to the block, they scarcely turned on the lights; fearing the approaching Russians, they strictly observed the blackout.

One day the nine men, in secret, sent us a canteen full of gold teeth. They said we should use them to bribe the blokova so that we would be transferred to another job. I didn't ask myself where they got the gold teeth from; I knew that they had put themselves in danger and done everything they could to save their daughters.

Meanwhile we were four girls and women from our village still left together in Auschwitz. One of the older women in this group led the negotiations with the blokova. The bribe worked, and she arranged for the four of us to work in a different place. In the last note I received from my father, it was written, "Tonight they are taking us to Majdanek, and there will be our graves. Mark my *yahrzeit* [anniversary of my death] on the 25th of the month of Elul." Today I know that in those days, the Majdanek extermination camp was already not operational, and my father may have meant a different place. But nevertheless, I never saw my father or heard from him again, and I never received any more notes from him.

My father was put to death.

We knew that during that month there were at least two uprisings in the crematorium. In the second one, we heard shots all night coming from there, and we found out later that many people were killed.

SEVENTY YEARS LATER

As a child, I understood that every home with Holocaust survivors had its own atmosphere, created by its occupants.

There were homes of Holocaust survivors where, as a child, I could smell the Holocaust in every corner as soon as I came in. The walls were soaked in sorrow, the furniture was forlorn, the light was gloomy, and the air was thick with the smell of smoke from the charred remains who lived there, who had indeed been saved from the fire and survived but were still smoking, and it seemed that the fire would never go out.

I suppose that every Holocaust survivor is like a charred log that will never really stop burning. But every survivor had his or her own fate, during the Holocaust and afterwards, and no survivor is like any other. My parents had the good fortune to find each other immediately after the war, fall in love, get married, start a family, immigrate to Israel, and build good lives there. Our home was one of happiness, tranquility, learning, creativity, culture, optimism, giving, volunteering, and joy of life. The strength and the happiness were the response to the Nazi enemy – we won, we survived, we have a state. We have a family, we are alive.

There were girls in my class whose parents were Holocaust

survivors, and their parents did not allow them to go on class trips out of fear for their safety. My older sisters also had to give up trips more than once for that reason. But I, who was born in a different period, went on whichever trips I wanted, and I even did my National Service guiding tours with the Society for the Preservation of Nature in Israel. My parents never tried to stop me; on the contrary, they placed great stock in a love of the Land of Israel, to which our people had returned after 2,000 years of exile.

There were girls I knew whose parents, Holocaust survivors, would not let them wear wooden clogs. Their tapping on the floor reminded the parents of the clogs in which the camp prisoners walked in snow, cold, and terror. As a teenager, I loved wearing wooden clogs, and I was never stopped from buying them and going around the house in them, despite the clatter they made. The value of ongoing and joyful life was important in our house, and I am full of appreciation and admiration for my parents who, by dint of the greatness of their personalities and with their own hands, lifted themselves out of the dust and made their lives glorious.

As a teenager, the greatest compliment someone could pay me was, "You don't seem like a child of Holocaust survivors." What did they think, that a second-generation Holocaust survivor is supposed to walk around hunched over? To speak with an East European accent? To wear old, patched clothes? To be as scrawny as a *muselmann*[25]? To be pale-faced with dark circles under the eyes? To be sad, pensive, and laden with sorrow?

---

25   *muselmann*: A Yiddish word that concentration camp inmates used to refer to an inmate who was resigned to his or her impending death.

Then no. My sisters and I were contented, happy, and free girls. We were girls who were well aware of the weight of the Holocaust, but did not let it stoop our shoulders.

My parents spoke Yiddish at home because it was comfortable for them to speak to each other in their mother tongue. They both also knew Hebrew very well. Every day after work my father studied Torah, and my mother also attended various Torah classes. She also attended free classes in the Land of Israel Studies department at the university. But at home, inside, they spoke Yiddish.

But I wanted us to be Israelis. After all, we beat the Holocaust! We beat the enemies! We live in the Land of Israel!

"Don't speak Yiddish!" I would cry every time they spoke between themselves in the language of the Exile.

I refused to learn the language and understand it. They spoke to me only in Hebrew. Outside of our home, they spoke only Hebrew in my presence. They understood my desire for us to be Israeli, and that we shouldn't be seen as Jews of the Exile.

And for me, even though as a child I refused to learn Yiddish, even though I resisted it and ran away from it, it still seeped into me without my noticing, and to this day I can understand many Yiddish words.

The common thread among all the homes of Holocaust survivors was the respect for food. In our home, too, no one threw away food. Every day my parents bought a loaf (or half a loaf) of fresh bread, but if some bread was still left from the previous day, they made sure to finish that first before slicing the fresh loaf.

In our building lived a family originally from Hungary, a husband and wife who were Holocaust survivors, and their daughter, two years older than me, who was my friend. I learned from her that it was possible to relate to food more casually. My friend would wait until her mother left the kitchen, sneak me in between the pots simmering on the gas range, lift a large pot lid, stick a spoon in, and taste the soup as it cooked.

"It's delicious!" she would swoon with pleasure. "You have to taste it!"

"Right from the pot?" I asked in shock the first time. I had never seen anything like that. In our home, food was a survival, life-or-death commodity. People eat because they have to. And one must finish everything on the plate! One masticates the chicken chew by chew, and again chew by chew, because one has to. I didn't like any food except sweets, but I was obligated to sit at the table and not get up until my plate was empty. And now, here was my friend sneaking a taste of soup, of her own free will, without anyone making her eat! She filled a spoon to overflowing with bubbling hot chicken soup and served it to me. I blew on the soup and swallowed it. I will never forget the flavor and aroma of that stolen spoonful of soup, soup that I ate without anyone forcing me, with laughter, not with the seriousness of existential survival. It took me years more to learn how to relate to food without complexes and, in parallel, to understand that my mother's dishes are the most delicious in the world.

"I have to show you something," that same friend said one day when her mother was out shopping. I was about 10 years old.

She led me to a closet on the porch of their house, rummaged through the drawers, and pulled out a large brown paper envelope. From it she took out about five black and white photographs.

"Who's that?!" I asked, studying the short, thin man in the photographs, who was seated in a glass cubicle, his shoulder hunched to one side, bespectacled, headphones on his ears, with a policeman sitting on either side of him. On another podium to the side of the picture was a man speaking into a microphone, but he didn't stand inside a glass cubicle.

"I have no idea," whispered my friend, listening to see if someone was at the door. "It must be connected to the Holocaust. That's a bad man from the Holocaust," she declared.

"How do you know that he is bad?"

"You can see he's bad," she answered. "He did something bad to the Jews in the Holocaust."

"And why do you have these photographs?"

"Don't know. But I saw my mother looking at them and crying."

Later I understood that this had been my first exposure to the Eichmann trial, which took place two years before I was born.

THE MILITARY TEXTILE MILL AT AUSCHWITZ

The gold teeth that the blokova Gizi received in the canteen pushed her to act on our behalf. She decided to help get us released from Block 16 and transferred to a different workplace. The most effective way she could do this was to get us, the four girls from Komját whose fathers worked in the sonderkommando, transferred to the lepers' block, the *Kretche-blok*.

First Gizi brought us some kind of stuff to rub on ourselves. I don't know what it was, but we spread it on our bodies. Within two or three days, red, itchy sores appeared under our skin.

We were taken out of Block 16, transferred to the *Kretche-blok*, and told not to scratch the sores. There they changed our clothes, and we never again wore blue dresses with white polka dots, but dresses made of a thick, bluish-gray fabric with stripes. There were several patterns of dresses for prisoners in Auschwitz, mostly of coarse bluish-gray fabric with narrow or wide stripes. From then on, whenever we took showers – something that happened only rarely – we were given dresses with a different pattern, with a different kind of stripes, but always a shade of gray-blue and a coarse texture.

We remained in the block that had been the leper hospital for five or six days. Other than the four of us, there were no other patients during those days. There was a fear that from there they might actually take us to be killed if something went wrong with the plans and someone decided that we were in fact lepers.

One day while we were in the lepers' block, I heard men quietly singing the *Rosh Hashana* prayers. I couldn't tell where the voices were coming from or who the men were, but their singing sent chills down my spine, along with an overwhelming longing for my family, the synagogue, and our village.

A doctor examined us and signed off on our transfer to a different camp and a new job. Apparently he had also been bribed and received some of the gold. We were sent to wash up, and from there to residential Block 22, in Lager B, and to a different job. We left the Lepers' Block on Thursday and were immediately sent to the new job. It was a few days before *Yom Kippur* (the Day of Atonement).

We came to the military textile mill called "Weberei"[26] where they taught us our job. We wove strong cables, which were used to lift supplies and equipment onto planes. The cables were made of strips of leather braided together with metal wires. They told us that the work had to be extremely precise.

At the factory, we were received by Halperin, the Jewish engineer from Munkács, who was 28 years old and knew my father. His family had run a towel factory in Munkács, and his job in the military textile mill in Auschwitz was to check the machines.

While Halperin was speaking with us, explaining our work at the factory, he lowered his voice, carefully pulled a note out

---

26 Apparently the reference is to the Schlesische Feinweberei factory that operated in Auschwitz from September 1944 until January 1945.

of his pocket, and handed it to Ruchi Klein. She read it silently and discovered that it was written by her father, who had also worked in the sonderkommando but had stayed alive. Of our nine fathers from Komjat who worked there, four had been executed, including my father, and five had been left alive – for the time being. While he was explaining our work, Halperin told us about the uprising that the crematorium workers had tried to organize.

"They made plans with the partisans," he told us, "and the partisans entered Auschwitz pretending to be doctors. They left a lot of vodka for the Germans to drink. Every Saturday night the Germans would have a party in the four-story building, and the soldiers would fall into a drunken stupor and sleep on the stairs. The plan was that after midnight, when everyone was drunk, the partisans would blow up the building with the Germans in it. There were supposed to be more than 1,000 German officers there, and they planned to booby-trap the crematorium, too, but the whole plan failed."

In the end, the uprising took place a week later, on October 7, 1944, but by then my father was already no longer among the living.

We were very agitated, but Halperin told us not to fear because it would be easier for us in this factory than in other places in Auschwitz.

The textile mill was part of a munitions factory that was partially staffed by non-Jewish workers from outside Auschwitz. They brought with them news from the outside, and sometimes their updates passed as rumors among the Jewish prisoners. Every day we went out with a large group of women to work at the textile mill.

We had to cut strips of leather one centimeter wide and weave them together with metal wires to create a cable four centimeters in width. One day I cut myself on the sharp shears, and the scar is visible on my fingers to this day. The kapos checked our work all the time, and anyone who didn't perform her task correctly received murderous lashes with the strip of leather.

Our new blokova was even worse than Gizi. It turned out that the worst things in Auschwitz had things even worse than they were. Here, too, there were roll calls every morning and evening in which we were counted to make sure that no one was missing. Except for being called out for roll call, we didn't move anywhere. The conditions in the block were just as bad as in the previous one, and there was no need to teach us the rules as we already knew them all too well.

Every day lunch was given out at the factory. It consisted of murky soup, without seasoning, with unidentifiable vegetables, including the peels, floating in it. Every five girls were given one bowl of soup, and they had to figure out how to divide it among themselves. It worked out that each one took about three swallows of soup. We were given the soup while we were working, and we drank it hastily. A kapo stood over us to make sure that we returned to work promptly.

Halperin brought me a dish known as a "*marinka*," which was made of three oval trays nested one inside the other. My father's name, Yakov Hershkovits, was engraved on the dish. I have no idea how, but my father had thought of everything and had managed to get this dish to Halperin in case I needed to store food. My friends also received such dishes.

A few days after we arrived at our jobs at the military textile mill, it was *Yom Kippur*. We were given lunch at the factory, but because we were fasting, we put the food in the marinka. In the evening we returned to the block in a wide file, in groups of five girls, and suddenly we heard from those marching before us that they were checking everyone to see if she had food in a marinka; anyone who did was being brutally beaten. My friends and I opened our marinkas and ate the food as we were walking, but the marinkas were still dirty. We were terrified that if they saw the remains of food, they would beat us to death, so we took off our underpants and used them to wipe the *marinkas*. It would be better to find a way to wash our underpants later or find other ones than to risk our lives.

October passed, November arrived, and it began to snow. There were windows on the roof of the textile mill that were never closed, and we worked underneath them. In addition to the freezing cold coming in from the open windows, snowflakes drifted in and settled on our shoulders as we sat working. We couldn't get up to shake off the snow, nor was there anywhere to shake it off, for if we had brushed it onto the floor we would have been beaten by the kapo. Thus we sat for days on end, from morning to evening, with snow on our shoulders, and worked. How much strength a girl has when she wants to survive . . .

In that period I didn't have shoes, for they kept getting stolen from me. Halperin brought me a pair of shoes, but when I woke up the next morning, I discovered that they had also been stolen while I was sleeping. That morning I was given wooden clogs, which were difficult to walk in, but for lack of other options I had to wear them. It began to snow, and anyone who tried to walk in clogs on the snow slipped and fell.

That day they rushed us out to the roll call, and I walked quickly while wearing the clogs. Suddenly one clog stuck in the snow, and in my great hurry I didn't manage to put my left foot back into the clog properly. My little toe remained outside the clog, but they were hurrying us so much that I couldn't stop to fix the shoe. I was forced to walk like that, with my little toe outside the clog, and it broke as I walked. I walked along sobbing with pain, but no one stopped to ask what had happened and if I needed help. There were moments in Auschwitz when each person was fighting for her own survival. It was hard for everyone, everyone was suffering from various illnesses and pains, and it was not always possible to help or even express solidarity with someone else's pain. That toe is crooked until today.

When we reached the factory, I told Halperin that my shoes had been stolen in the night. A few days later he brought me another pair, and they too were stolen that night. He brought me a third pair, and those I kept on my feet all the time, and thus managed to hold onto them for a long time. Another time Halperin managed to sneak me a pair of woolen knee socks that helped a bit to keep me warm. At another opportunity he sneaked in a jacket for me.

Once in a while Halperin would secretly bring me items, like a little pocket knife or some thread, which he said my father had sent me. Since the prisoners did not have any property of their own, a barter system flourished; prisoners in Auschwitz would "sell" each other items that had come into their possession, with the price being a slice of bread. It was impossible to expect a 16-year-old girl to become a big dealer, but still, once or twice I managed to sell things for slices of bread.

One day they took the girls of our block to the showers. As we stood in line waiting to go inside, we heard that doctors were waiting in the showers to conduct a selection. The rumor was that they were taking aside all those who had festering sores and sending them to their death so that they wouldn't infect others with their sores. Given the unhygienic conditions and lack of nourishment, we all had festering sores on various parts of our bodies. The girls said that apparently half of us would be taken out to be killed.

We were terrified. I thought to myself – how can one be saved from such a selection? Up until now I had been saved by Heaven's mercy and because of my father's merits, but also by resourcefulness.

I looked ahead to the girls in front of us. One of them carried her shoes tied by their laces over her bare shoulder and held her clothes in a bundle in her hand, as we all did. Suddenly I noticed that her shoe, covered with mud, was touching the back of another friend, spattering her with mud and hiding a festering sore that she had on her back. I immediately suggested to my friends that we cover our sores with mud.

And so we did. My close friends and I quickly covered each other's sores with mud. When our turn came, we all went into the shower, and thus we were saved from this selection.

Not to Be the Fifth in the Row

The night passed.
It is already morning but the light has not returned.
Everything is gloomy, dark and foreign,
Everything is rigid, frozen and cold.
We are standing all night.
Our bodies have no weight.
Out of every five – one is extra.
Sad, gray and dulled,
There are no senses, everything is confused.
There is no justice and no anger, everything has been
cancelled.
The body is weakened and almost surrenders.
Then, from somewhere – some wind of soul
Awakens to do battle.
Life has strength and a goal:
Not to be the fifth in the row.
Because to be the fifth is the end.
It is beyond one's control, it is death in the crematorium.

MIRACULOUS RESCUE FROM THE HOSPITAL

Every morning we marched in rows of five to the military textile mill, and every evening we marched back. As we walked, we would pass other groups of girls on their way to other work sites in Auschwitz.

One day, in the group of girls coming towards us, I spotted my cousin Beilcho! Beilcho Gelb was the daughter of my uncle Shmil-David Gelb. They lived in the village of Khust, close to our village, and I was good friends with her and her sisters.

Beilcho arrived at Auschwitz before us, as I found out later. Before Passover of 1944, while working in the sewing workshop in Khust, she suddenly heard Jews being arrested in the street. She ran away from the workshop and managed to reach Budapest. She thought she would be safe there, but she was arrested in the city and sent immediately to Auschwitz.

Beilcho looked at me and I at her. We couldn't do anything more. Both of us saw in each other's eyes the joy of our meeting, and also the sorrow that our other family members had not survived.

The next day I asked the girls in my group to let me stand at the end of the row. Beilcho also stood at the end of her row, and thus we could nod greetings to each other. Every morning we would pass by each other, and sometimes we managed to whisper a word or two. One time Beilcho asked me if I had seen her sisters in Auschwitz. I answered that I had not seen them.

But one morning, as we marched to work via Lager C, I suddenly saw Beilcho's three sisters: Blimcho, Ruzci, and Eyvi! Blimcho was seven years older than me, Beilcho four years older, Ruzci a year older, and Eyvi a year younger.

The girls of my generation were beautiful, blond, and blue-eyed, but at that moment they looked awful. Their hair was shorn, their eyes were nothing but black holes, and they were emaciated and looked sick and weak. I thought to myself that I must also look like that. And yet, we knew that the conditions in Lager C were worse than where we were. People said that prisoners there were given very little food, and that they would sell their clothes for half a slice of bread.

The next morning, when I passed Beilcho with my line, I whispered to her, "I saw your sisters in Lager C!" My cousin's eyes lit up with joy, mixed with worry.

From that day, Beilcho began to look out for her sisters in Lager C. At that time, she worked sorting clothes, so she was able to occasionally slip an object out of a suitcase, whenever the kapo was not looking. She prepared little packages for her sisters, wrapped in thin headscarves. Every once in a while, when we were passing each other, she would throw a package towards me, and when I would pass through Lager C I would throw the package to her sisters. Once the package contained two cloves of garlic, once two sugar cubes or squares of choco-late, and once a screw that they could sell to another prisoner for half a slice of bread.

I knew that what I was doing was dangerous. If the kapo saw me, I would likely get a beating or some worse punishment. But after everything I had been through in Auschwitz, after they killed my parents and my little brothers, the only thing left in me were the values of good deeds and giving that I had absorbed from my home. Helping someone else reminded me that I was still a human being. And so I passed little packages and notes of encouragement from Beilcho to her sisters.

One morning one of the soldiers saw me catch the scarf that Beilcho threw me. Before I had a chance to say anything, the soldier punched me hard in the forehead. I do not know if she was German or Ukrainian, but she and those like her were very strong. The force of the blow knocked me to the ground, my head hit a stone, and I suffered a second blow to my left temple. I lost consciousness.

When I opened my eyes again, I saw that I was lying on a bed, covered with a white sheet. I understood that I was in the "hospital." The place was called "hospital" even though we had all heard that prisoners were not treated there, but rather subjected to medical experiments under the direction of Dr. Josef Mengele, the diabolical doctor. I had never before been in the "hospital" block in Auschwitz. Everyone I knew who was sent there never returned, and I thought my end had come. From here one went to the gas chambers, or remained and suffered horrendous pain as the subject of cruel experiments from which one was also likely to die.

I looked out the windows and saw that the sun was setting. I realized that I had been unconscious for an entire day. My head throbbed terribly. I had never had such a splitting headache. Every bone in my head hurt. I asked myself how I could get out of there safely.

Suddenly a woman in a white coat entered. On her head she wore a nurse's cap embroidered with the symbol of the Red Cross. She looked at me in amazement, clapped her hands, and said, "Blimcho!"

Blima was my dear mother, who was already at that time no longer among the living.

I said to the woman, "I am Suri, Blimcho's daughter."

The woman's mouth dropped open. She went out and then came back in, waiting a moment to make sure that no one was standing near us, and told me where she knew my mother from. Her name was Chana Shmilovitz, and she had grown up in Komjat and had been a childhood friend of my mother's. After her marriage, she and her husband moved to Belgium. The Germans conquered Belgium in the middle of the war, and Chana was sent to Auschwitz around 1942. At first she had been a regular prisoner, and somehow she ended up a nurse. She had children, but she didn't know their fate, nor that of her husband.

From all the excitement, fear, and pain, I began to cry. I couldn't understand how Chana, who had never seen me, had seen my mother in me.

Chana told me not to cry and asked me to tell her how I ended up in the "hospital." I told her in brief my history up to that day. I told her that my mother, father, and five brothers had perished in Auschwitz, that my baby sister had died in Komjat, and that I was the only surviving member of my whole family. I told her that I did not want to die.

"Don't worry," Chana whispered. "You won't die today. I'm going to get you out of here. You're going back to the block you came from. Trust me."

Chana called a Jewish prisoner who served as a courier, delivering mail and packages throughout Auschwitz. These couriers were called "*läuferin*" ("lauf" means "run"). By virtue of their duties, they were allowed to enter everywhere in Auschwitz. Chana told the läuferin that I was to accompany her on her rounds, and when we reached Lager B, my block, she was to leave me there.

The läuferin began to run, and I with her. That evening I went with her to every place she went on her delivery rounds. At every camp we passed along the way, she said that I was accompanying her, and thus they allowed me to move freely.

Finally we reached my block, but the girls had not yet returned from work. The blokova came out, the läuferin told her something, and the blokova said to me, "Sit outside until everyone comes back."

The läuferin left and the blokova went back inside the block. I remained alone outside, weak, shaking with fear, cold, and with a splitting headache, but I had been saved from the "hospital." Snow was falling, and I had nothing on but a dress, without a sweater or coat. I leaned my aching head against the wall of the block and dozed off. As soon as the girls arrived and lined up for roll call, I joined them for the evening count. When roll call ended, we entered the block and went to sleep.

Early the next morning I was dizzy and nauseous, and didn't know where I was. Very likely I was suffering from a concussion. I couldn't tell the blokova that I didn't feel well and ask for a day off work, because such a request would be like asking to die or to be sent back into Mengele's clutches. Dizzy and weak, I got out of bed, stood with everyone in the roll call and went with them to work. The girls told Halperin that the German soldier had struck me in the head, and he felt sorry for me and brought me soup in a marinka.

Halperin was eventually released from Auschwitz, moved to the United States, and raised a family there. His nephew lived in Israel, and I met with him and his wife and asked him to thank his uncle across the seas for all the goodness and kindness he showed us.

I never saw Chana Shmilovitz again, and I don't know what happened to her, although the four daughters of my uncle from the Gelb side – Blimcho, Beilcho, Ruczi, and Eyvi – did survive the Holocaust. Except for Beilcho, who lived in the United States, they all moved to Israel and raised families.

In Auschwitz, we were all links in a chain of souls who saved each other.

MEMORIES OF THE ETIQUETTE LESSONS

The starvation in Auschwitz and the terrible living conditions led us to behavior that did not follow normal rules of politeness. When you are occupied with trying to survive the next minute, you eat with your hands, wipe your nose on your sleeve, and do other unacceptable things. To hold onto my humanity, I would occasionally ponder the etiquette lessons that I had taken two years earlier, together with my sisters Ruchi and Faige, with *Lernen Fraulein Munczi* (the teacher Miss Munczi).

The lessons took place at the home of Natan Hershkovits, my father's cousin. His wife Shprintze was very wealthy, dressed elegantly, and had many servants. They lived in Urdo, a village next to Komjat, with their 10 children, including Golde and Miriam, who were about my age. The lessons began when I was 12, Ruchi 10 and Faige 4, and continued for two years, once a week.

It all started when the Hershkovits family from Urdo took pity on a woman named Munczi, a cosmetician from Belgium, whose husband was drafted into the Hungarian army; she, left without papers, was forced to return to Urdo. To earn a living, she posted an advertisement that she was offering etiquette lessons. And who would want to teach their daughters etiquette in the middle of a war? Only a family of millionaires.

Lernen Munczi began teaching Golde and Miriam Hershkovitz etiquette on Sundays. The girls, however, didn't want to go and they would giggle and run away. Their mother came up with the idea that my sisters and I would join the lessons, and thus her daughters would want to stay rather than run away. Although my little sister Faige was only four at the time, Mrs. Hershkovits said that it was good to start learning etiquette at a young age.

Every Sunday a carriage would be sent from Urdo to our house in Komjat to pick up my sisters Ruchi and Faige, another cousin named Sheyve, and me for the etiquette lessons with Miss Munczi. On the way, the carriage passed through a forest. In the winter there were warm blankets in the carriage, and a hot stone would be placed on the armrest so that our journey would be comfortable and pleasant.

The etiquette lessons took place from 1940 until 1942, while a terrible war was being fought in Europe. Miss Munczi taught us how to sit at the table, and how to hold a cup. She taught us that tea is drunk from a glass cup and black coffee from a small mug, while coffee with milk is drunk from a large mug. The saucer must match the cup. She taught us how to set the table and how to eat properly with a knife and fork.

Miss Munczi was well groomed, always dressed in beautiful clothes, and always looked elegant, even though she had no income other than the etiquette lessons at the Hershkovits family. She had a 12-year-old daughter, and the two of them were given lunch every Sunday in the Hershkovits home.

At first we would giggle during the lessons, but my mother

asked us to respect Miss Munczi, so we restrained ourselves and tried to be serious. Sometimes in the winter we didn't want to make the trip, but my mother said we were doing a *mitzvah*. She said to me, "Imagine if your brother Eliezer wouldn't have any lunch today." Therefore I was always considerate and, understanding that it was important for us to go, I encouraged my younger sisters to go willingly.

On Sabbath evenings, my sisters and I would teach our brothers what we had learned that week. For example, we would demonstrate how to walk erect with a book on one's head, and how to walk without scuffing one's heels.

Now in Auschwitz, I remembered those lessons and weeped. My dear sisters Ruchi and Faige were no longer among the living. Most of the Hershkovits family from the village of Urdo had also perished, and Fraulein Munczi and her daughter had also been sent to the gas chambers as soon as we arrived in Auschwitz. Etiquette was the last thing on our minds. Most of the time I didn't even have water to wash my dirty hands with before eating the slice of bread I was given. Sometimes I did have water, and I was able to say the blessing aloud, and the girls near me would answer "Amen," but then I would have nothing to wipe my hands on except the stinking dress that covered my body.

The Shame of Starvation

I did not eat my fill of bread,
I drank a measure of moldy water.
I was always hungry.
I did not sleep on a bed,
I wore an ugly, evil, striped garment,
I did not bathe, did not comb my hair,
And did not laugh.
I did not know towel or soap,
I did not hold a toothbrush,
I did not change underwear or clothes.

I do not know how I made it through
So much evil.
Do not ask me, for I do not know.
I have no answers.
It was terribly hard –
Because I did not dream, either.
But the shame of starvation, so it seems,
I conquered.

SEVENTY YEARS LATER

Holocaust Remembrance Day, which was first introduced in Israel when I was 11 or 12, brought about a revolution in my life.

I came home from school in the afternoon. My parents weren't home, but I knew that they would be back any minute from work and errands, so I innocently sat down in front of the television to await their return. Nothing had prepared me for the sight that met my eyes. The Holocaust in all its nakedness was presented on the screen, without censoring, without cover-up, without concealment, without any prettying up. Dead children, naked fleshless skeletons loaded on carts and dumped into pits; human skeletons crouching in the streets, half-dead, as emaciated, pale people passed by without stopping to care for them, succumbing to their own despair, corpses dropped in a row, one on top of the other, with flies hovering over them, as if no one cared about the presence of death.

It was these black and white photographs that immortalized humanity's darkest and most despicable moments.

My jaw dropped in shock. At that moment, the Holocaust took on a face and a form, and was revealed as the very embodiment of cruelty.

I sat rigid, glued to the chair. I couldn't breathe. I couldn't tear my eyes away from the images. The truth struck me with terrible pain, exploded in my face, and made it palpably clear to me what happened in the Holocaust.

I shed no tears. I understood everything, but the pain was too great for tears.

When my parents returned home I turned off the television. I didn't want them to see the images. I didn't want them to experience the pain that I myself was feeling. I wanted to protect them from the pain.

I didn't sleep a wink that night, nor the following few nights. I faced the chilling knowledge that 6,000,000 Jews were murdered thus, including my grandparents, aunts, uncles, and cousins.

As the days passed, the pain and sorrow over the death of my family members became part of my life. I saw how my parents lifted themselves out of the bereavement, how they knew how to rejoice, laugh, and lead normal lives alongside the trauma, pain, and loss. I knew that I had to be strong like them. Life was good and beautiful, and the good must triumph! I knew that my parents were strong for me and my sisters and for the new grandchildren born to them, and I decided that I, too, would be strong – for them.

A year passed, and again it was Holocaust Memorial Day Eve. Again I was alone at home in the afternoon in front of the television. Again the screen showed black-and-white footage filmed during the Holocaust, documenting the horrific crimes that man committed against man. The images were hard to watch. I knew that again I wouldn't be able to sleep for several nights, but I forced myself to sit and watch. You have to know exactly what went on there, I told myself. It's the least you can do to honor your parents and the memory of your family.

Thus I sat in front of the television on subsequent years as well.

With the passing of time, the television programs on Holocaust Memorial Day underwent a change. They became softer, more moderate. Perhaps educators and psychologists had become enlightened and decided, correctly, that it was not proper to show the monstrous and nauseating film clips publicly on a screen. On television they began to show a Holocaust that was more "esthetic," more refined, in color rather than black and white, with today's perspective on the terrible past, at a distance, and with compassion for the viewer.

As a second-generation daughter, the Holocaust is part of my life. As an adult, it seems that not a day goes by without some thought about my family who perished in the Holocaust, about my parents who were saved, or about the Holocaust itself. The survivors and their families have no need of Memorial Day to jog their memories, yet they draw encouragement and strength from the knowledge that on that day the entire country stops and remembers.

When my children were small, I didn't know how to relate to them on that day. Should we bequeath to them customs of mourning and sorrow? Should we forbid them to laugh and rejoice on that day? With the years, I came to understand that the Holocaust is part of my children's lives as well, as third-generation survivors, and that I should not decide for them how to behave on Memorial Day; the Holocaust flows in their blood, too.

On the night before Holocaust Memorial Day, we light a memorial candle and place next to it a list of our relatives who perished, with pictures of a few of them. Of all our relatives, photographs remain only of my paternal grandparents, Sheindel and Levi Yitzhak Leibovits; of my father's two sisters, Etu and Gitu; and of my Grandma Blima Hershkovits in her youth, standing next to her mother Chana-Devora and her sister Sheyve. The faces of the rest of our family members murdered in Auschwitz will remain forever hidden from our view.

On some Memorial Days I lead discussion groups on the Holocaust in our family, and then the whole following week I am struck with a kind of paralysis, unable to do anything, barely breathing.

On Memorial Days when I am not lecturing about the Holocaust, I am calmer and feel more than ever the need to envelop my children in warmth and protection. In my childhood, any time my mother wanted to make me happy and envelop me in warmth, she would make me blintzes that she called "*palacsinta*," which tasted like a sweet cake soaked in honey. Her mother had also made the same palacsinta for her and her siblings, with the same flavor, and now my mother makes them for her grandchildren and great-grandchildren. I continue the family tradition, and usually make palacsinta on the eve of Holocaust Memorial Day, since it is a food that is all about comfort and warmth, love, and security.

"I am sure that our relatives who perished in the Holocaust

would be happy to know that we survived," I tell my children, "that we are living in the Land of Israel, that we have enough food, that we are happy and alive, that we are eating palacsinta. And yes, we will eat for them, for if someone had told them then, on their way to the gas chambers in Auschwitz, that their daughter and sister, son and brother – Suri Hershkovits and Shuli Leibovits – would be saved, would get married, would move to Israel, would raise a beautiful family, and that their grandchildren would eat palacsinta in the Land of Israel, maybe, just maybe, a last smile would cross their lips. They would have wanted to know that we survived. That we triumphed."

And there are days when I think to myself – maybe my present life is all fiction, an illusion, a dream. Maybe the truth is that I am in fact a woman lying at this moment on a crowded board in Auschwitz, sleeping a frenzied night's sleep and dreaming my life. In another moment it will be dawn, a whistle will sound and I will wake up. "Hurry! Hurry! Get off the boards and line up for zahlappel!"

SUGAR CUBES IN AUSCHWITZ

Day followed day, hunger followed hunger, cold followed cold, and it was the month of December — and with it the holiday of *Hanukah*.[27] Later, I heard of Jewish prisoners who managed, by the most circuitous means, to light *Hanukah* candles in Auschwitz. They pulled threads out of the blankets to make wicks, dipped them in margarine, bought a cigarette from someone in exchange for something else, and thus lit candles. But we didn't manage to light candles.

We continued to live in horrific conditions of want and illness and to suffer torture and humiliation. Everyone was sick and infected because of the lack of hygiene. At night and in the morning it was usually snowing, and we were not adequately dressed for the bitter cold. Sometimes at noon a pale sun shone and melted the snow a bit, but at night more snow fell, and all of Auschwitz was covered in frost and ice.

One morning we arrived at the military textile mill only to find that all the blocks of the mill no longer existed. They had been completely dismantled. Halperin had also disappeared.

---

27   *Hanukah*: An eight-day festival celebrating the rededication of the Temple after the Jewish victory over the Greeks. Candles are lit each evening of the festival.

They told us that the specialists at the munitions factory had been transferred to Germany. In fact, all of Auschwitz looked like it was in the process of being dismantled. We heard that they had blown up the crematorium earlier, and we heard that the Germans were covering up evidence, that they were covering up the fire pits with sand and running away to Germany. For weeks we had seen them taking out piles of documents, brushing off a bit of snow, and burning them.

The block where we slept was about an hour's walk from the munitions factory. They marched us to another block, a large hangar, brought us inside, and told us to wait. There was no place to sit there; it was cold, the wind was blowing, and rain and perhaps even snow was falling. There were some tens of thousands of prisoners left in Auschwitz in those days, out of the hundreds of thousands that had been there earlier, before most of the prisoners were sent to Germany. Most of the German soldiers had also returned to Germany, since the Russian army was approaching Auschwitz. The munitions factories were closed and there was nothing for us to do. I suppose that in theory, they could have taken all the remaining prisoners out to be shot, but they didn't, perhaps because the Nazis still needed forced labor and intended to use us in the future.

For two or three days we did nothing. The guards weren't Germans, but rather Polish or Ukrainian soldiers who gave us commands in Polish. Rumor had it that they were non-Jewish prisoners whom the Germans had released from prisons in Poland and the Ukraine in order to watch over us while they themselves escaped to Germany, until all the Auschwitz prisoners would be sent to Germany.

At a certain point, so that we would not sit idle, the guards decided to give us a pointless and useless task: to move very heavy beds from one place to another. They were wooden beds, with two boards, on which 14 girls slept every night.

They began to arrange us in groups of six girls, and they placed a heavy wooden bed on the shoulders of each group. I was on the right side of the two girls in the middle of the six, and the bed was placed on my left shoulder. A fight broke out among the girls and they began shouting, because they didn't know where the best place to stand was. There were girls who collapsed under the weight of the bed, and the guards kept shouting instructions in Polish.

We were emaciated, hungry, and frozen with cold, but we had no choice. The command was given, and we began to march with the beds on our shoulders. We marched for hours, until nightfall. At night we slept in a large warehouse, on the same beds that we had dragged, and we were given almost no food or drink. The next morning they came back and made us go outside and repeat the same scenario. Thus we spent several days walking with the beds on our shoulders. It was an indescribable nightmare. In time I came to know the route well, since it was lined with numbered markers, and I knew how much of the route we had covered and how much we still had to go.

On one of those days, while we were marching with the heavy beds on our shoulders, I felt that I had reached the end of my strength. I felt that the end had come, and I was very sad. I knew that I was the last remaining member of our family, and I grieved to think that no remnant of our family would be left. I walked on stumbling legs, slipping in wooden clogs, with the bed on my shoulder, on muddy earth mixed with snow, and I feared that if I fell on this stretch of road, I would be covered with dirt and they wouldn't want to help me up. I thought it would be better to fall farther on, where the road was paved, so that they could help me get up again. I addressed the Master of the Universe: "How can it be that we are being punished so? What did we do to deserve this?"

I knew that one was supposed to say "*Sh'ma Yisrael*"[28] when dying, but I didn't know if I was supposed to shout it or say it quietly. I didn't know if I should say it already, or only when I fell. I slipped into a sort of stupor, understanding that in another moment I was going to crumple to the ground and they would step on me. We were all exhausted and weak, and when someone fell, the others would step on her and trample her body.

With supreme mental effort, I continued marching, saying to myself – a little more, try to keep going, don't fall.

Suddenly I saw a large group of men walking alongside us. They were dressed in warm civilian clothes, not prisoners' uniforms. They took off their hats and called in several languages, "Partisans! Partisans! Where are you from?" I thought they were partisans who had been taken prisoner and brought to Auschwitz.

They shouted in several languages, "Are there Jews here?" "*Hanukah, Hanukah!*" "Christmas!" and threw us scarves and sweaters, but it was hard to catch them while walking with the

---

28   *Sh'ma Yisrael* (Hear O Israel. . .): In Jewish tradition, a person says this prayer)Deut. 6:4) when he or she is about to die: "Hear O Israel, the Lord our God, the Lord is One."

beds on our shoulders.

Suddenly one of them yelled in my direction, "You, girl, the little one," and threw me a brown men's handkerchief with its four corners tied together. My right hand was free, and I managed to catch the package.

The partisans yelled at us, "Hang on. The Russians are already here. They have crossed the Vistula River!"

Then they passed us and continued on their way.

While continuing to march with the bed on my shoulders, I used my teeth and my free hand to untie the knots in the handkerchief. To my amazement, I discovered that it held large white cubes of sugar. I stuck one in my mouth. I couldn't pass any to my friends, since their heads were hidden under the bed and we were far apart from each other. I began to chew the sugar cube. At first my throat was so dry that I couldn't swallow, but after a minute my mouth was filled with sweetness, and the dryness passed. The feeling of sweetness spread through my whole body. Finally I could breathe. The pains in my stomach also passed as though touched by a magic wand. I ate some 20 sugar cubes, one after another, and I felt my strength returning. The sugar cubes revived me and returned my will and ability to survive.

At dusk, when we reached the storeroom and lowered the beds from our shoulders, all the girls attacked me and grabbed the kerchief with the dozens of sugar cubes that still remained. I kept aside four sugar cubes in my hand, but the girls fell on me, pried my hand open, and took those, too.

Later that night, when we lay down to sleep on the beds, I

thought about the partisans' words. At that moment, I didn't care about the approaching Russians. I wanted a bowl of soup, I wanted to be home, I wanted to find someone from my family who was still alive, but I knew that I had no home to return to, and that no one would be waiting for me with a cup of tea or hot soup. Thoughts of liberation brought both joy and sorrow intertwined, and were beyond my understanding at that moment.

I thought of the partisans' kindness in throwing clothing and food to us, and of the partisan who threw the sugar cubes to me and, ostensibly, saved my life in doing so. For my sake he gave up the sugar cubes, as well as a handkerchief, a valuable commodity in the extermination camp. I don't know if he was aware that he had saved a wretched young woman by his action.

His gesture reminded me that even in the midst of the Hell we were in, in the deepest depths, a human soul can rise up and extend a helping hand. Humanity can be evil, but human beings can also be good, and every individual is given the right to choose.

I Shall Not Die, But Live

Five women eating soup from one bowl, with no spoon.
They drink the bitter black tea without batting an eyelash.
They tear the piece of bread with their hands,
For there is no knife in the accursed place,
And they debate whether to finish the slice all at once,
Or leave a bite or a crumb for tomorrow.
Without love and without comforts, just suffering and more
suffering,
I am alone, orphaned, in the midst of a great crowd.
I want to cry silently and feel the longings for yesterday,
Because the new day is always worse than all the rest.
In the morning I wished it would be evening.
In the evening I longed for the morning to come.
Sometimes I thought that it would never come to an end.
The suffering would never finish and the sun would never
come out of hiding.
The moon would never come out to light the gray skies.

Suddenly a new spirit of life rained on me from the heavens.
The spirit was clear and strong, brightening the eyes,
Straightened the bent spine, smoothed out the wrinkles.
I would say – resurrection of the dead.
Then I knew I had a mission,
To bear witness to everything that happened here.

I shall not die, but live –
And declare the works of the Lord!
I will recount how my Lord saved me from Hell
And shout out loud to the world: "The Jewish People Lives!"

SETTING OUT ON THE DEATH
MARCH TO GERMANY

In the following weeks I continued to be weak and starving, and my physical condition deteriorated steadily. At the beginning of January I felt awful. My body was burning up with fever. A nurse came, touched my face, and said, "You're going to the hospital now."

They brought me into a block that was also called a "hospital," but it was different from the previous "hospital" from which I had been rescued. This one was a regular block with bunk beds for female prisoners who were ill. The German doctors, including Mengele, had already run away back to Germany, and the patients were cared for by Jewish, or Polish and Ukrainian, nurses who were themselves prisoners in the camp. They had very few resources available to treat the many patients, and many prisoners breathed their last breaths there. But still the place was called a "hospital."

In the hospital block were other girls who were sick like me, and among them I discovered three girls from Hungary who were cousins. The first was named Piri and the second Irene Freider; I don't remember the third one's name. I befriended them immediately, but we stopped speaking Yiddish among ourselves because in the midst of all the tumult there, it had happened that Polish partisans came in, sought out Jews, and killed them purely out of anti-Jewish hatred. I was in the hospital for about a week. My fever went down and I began getting out of bed, but I still felt weak and my legs were shaky. In that block I was surrounded by sick people; everyone felt terrible and many were crying. From a distance we could hear explosions and the sounds of war, and we understood that the Russian front was very close.

On Thursday, January 18, 1945, the remaining German commanders and soldiers in Auschwitz began to evacuate the camp in a hurry. At that time there were about 58,000 prisoners in the camp, and the orders were to take us all to Germany by foot. On that Thursday they got us all out of bed, the sick and the recovering, and told us all to go outside for a march to Germany.

The men brought blankets, which looked clean and in good condition, apparently taken from the equipment storerooms of the German officers. One woman climbed up on the stone barrier around the heater in the middle of the block and shouted, "Attention please! Everyone tear off pieces of the blankets, wrap them around your feet instead of shoes and thus we will set out on our way."

They gave me a blanket and told me to go outside. I went outside, wrapped myself in the blanket and looked around. Everything was covered in snow. It was very cold and a blustery wind stung my face. They arranged us in rows of five, in a long line. I put on wooden clogs, but I knew I wouldn't be able to walk more than five steps in the snow without slipping. I didn't understand how to make shoes out of the blanket, as the woman had proposed. I had no scissors, and I didn't know how I would manage to tear a thick wool blanket. I stood in the row and looked all around me, wondering what I should do.

I looked towards the entrance to the hospital block, Block 22, and I saw a young woman getting out of line, running towards the entrance, and trying to get inside. A uniformed soldier, apparently Ukrainian, stood at the entrance. The soldier struck the girl hard, knocked her down in the snow, and sent her back to stand in the row. Sobbing, the poor girl returned to her row.

We continued to stand there, waiting, and it was so cold that I forgot that someone had just been beaten for trying to go into the block. I got out of line and, with the blanket on my head, hurried towards the block. To my great fortune, the Ukrainian soldier turned her head at that moment and didn't notice me.

When I came into the block, a woman named Yulan rushed up to me, telling me that she was a Jew, married to a Gentile. She asked me, "What are you doing here? Don't stand in the entrance. Quick, go lie down."

I told her, "I came to take the blanket that was on my bed, so that I would be warmer on the march to Germany."

Yulan looked at me with pity and said, "In your condition you'll never get to any Germany. Go in the corner quickly, pull a blanket over your head, and hide."

I did as she instructed. I pushed my way into the corner of one of the lower bunks, covered myself with a blanket, and fell asleep. I slept a deep, unbroken sleep, without anyone bothering me.

I awoke in a panic. My body was bathed in sweat and I was

burning up with fever. I was shaking and didn't know where I was. It was silent in the block, with only an occasional moan from one of the beds. Some of the beds were piled with dead bodies. Little by little, other girls – who had hidden like me – started to come out of hiding, and I discovered Piri, Irene, and their cousin on the beds. They had stayed in bed the whole time, being unable to stand up.

I figured out that it was Thursday evening. I looked out the window. It was dark outside, and no one was there. It turned out that the march to Germany, which was to become known as the "Death March," had left without us. Only a few of us, some 8,000, were left in Auschwitz.

I was very hungry and wanted to drink a cup of tea, but there was no one to bring us food or drink. My fever went up again, and, feeling terribly sick, I fell asleep.

All that night we heard explosions around us, as though we were in the middle of a battlefield. We saw flashes of the explosions through the windows, and we were terrified that they would bomb Auschwitz too, everyone who remained in the camp.

Friday passed in a blur, with no food or drink. When the Sabbath began, Irene said that this time we wouldn't light Sabbath candles, so that they wouldn't know that we were Jews. I didn't understand what she was talking about. Up until that time I had never seen a woman in Auschwitz light candles on Sabbath eve. But it turned out that there were such women who, in certain circumstances, had managed to do so.

On Sabbath morning my fever went down somewhat, but I

was so weak that I could barely stand. I couldn't stop shivering. On the floor of the block I found some cast-off clothing and a pair of shoes, but very quickly I lay back down in bed. Gradually it dawned on me that if I had set out on that march, I wouldn't have survived the first kilometer.

I hadn't touched food or drink since Thursday, and I have no idea how I survived. The will to live was apparently stronger than anything else. Fortunately for us, two Ukrainian women came into Block 22 during the Sabbath and, amazingly, they were good to us. Outside on the snow they arranged bricks, then dragged out beds, broke them up into boards, lit a bonfire, and placed over it a pot filled with snow. They gave out warm melted snow to all the patients in the block, and I, too, received a metal bowl with warm water in it. I drank it and felt a bit better.

On Sunday some drunken soldiers came in to the block to see if any Jews remained there. Apparently they were German deserters who wanted to justify their desertion by claiming that they went back to look for Jews who remained in the camp.

The Ukrainian women who were managing the block treated us well. They knew that some of us were Jews, but one of them said to the soldiers, "No, what do you think? Jews? In our block? We're Ukrainians!" She gave the soldiers something to drink and they went on their way.

Throughout that day we continued drinking warm snowmelt and I felt myself getting stronger. I could get out of bed and walk. Outside it was hailing, making a terrible racket, and after that it began to snow. Someone said that the snow was a meter deep.

On Monday I heard that people who remained in the camp had managed to break into a bread warehouse somewhere in Auschwitz. Although still very weak, I decided that I had to go with people to bring back bread for my friends and me. They were still in bed, unable even to stand up.

One of my friends among the patients gave me some shoes, another gave me pants and brought me other articles of clothing, and I went out into the snow, following everyone else's tracks to the warehouse. The huge warehouse was full of bread. I took three large, square loaves and, hugging them to myself with great excitement, headed back through the snow towards the block. Suddenly one of the loaves fell into the snow and I tried to bend over and pick it up. Seemingly such a simple act – to bend down and pick up a fallen loaf of bread – but I was so weak that I couldn't manage it. With great sorrow I left it in the snow and returned to the block carrying the two remaining loaves.

We tore the bread by hand, divided it among everyone, and tried to eat. We chewed and chewed, but experienced intense pains in our cheeks and throats. We couldn't swallow. We crumbled the bread into tiny pieces and gradually managed to eat, bite by bite.

We heard that people were looking for additional warehouses of the Germans' food and equipment. Someone said that they had found enormous warehouses with fish and meat, but the Germans, before their exodus, had opened the warehouses so that the meat would spoil. They had blown up other warehouses with grenades, but still, there were some intact warehouses left.

In the evening we were told that they had opened an

equipment warehouse, and I decided to go there. That one held young people's clothing, and I collected warm pants, shirts, and good-quality sweaters. I put on two or three layers and brought clothes to my friends as well.

When I returned, Irene had already lit a fire outside and boiled snow, so we ate our fill of bread and drank hot water.

Someone said, "We're liberated, we've been liberated from Auschwitz," but we all looked at her, uncomprehending. What did she mean by "We've been liberated?" It was difficult to grasp that the nightmare of Auschwitz might be over.

I went to sleep, feeling full for the first time in almost a year. I thought about what had been said, about the fact that we had apparently been liberated from Auschwitz. But with that thought, I began to cry and my soul began to ache. I knew that I had nowhere to go back to.

At the same time, new fears began to stir in our hearts. Up until now we had heard the explosions and sounds of fighting between the Germans and the Russians only at a distance, but suddenly that night the explosions ceased and a threatening quiet fell outside.

That night we all cried, thinking that the Germans had defeated the Russians. We feared the worst of all – that the next day the Germans would return and shoot everyone who was still left in the camp.

THE DREAM THAT I WILL NEVER FORGET

Early Tuesday morning, five days after we had been left alone in Auschwitz, I dreamed that I was lying in a bed. Not a board in Auschwitz, but a normal bed. I dreamed that I was waking up and sitting up in bed because they were telling me, "Your father is coming! Your father is coming!"

I saw my father coming towards me, nicely dressed, wearing a hat, his face adorned with a beard, like it was when we were still at home. He was in a good mood, with a smile on his face, like always, for my father wore a perennial smile. He was wearing a winter coat with many pockets. From one of the pockets he pulled out a green bottle that had once had black beer, gave it to me and said, "Drink, drink, *Tochterko*." My father often called me by that name in Yiddish, making the word "*tochter*" (daughter) into an affectionate nickname.

I drank and drank.

As a child I had been slender, and my father would often urge me to eat, sitting with me at the table and convincing me with a smile to swallow a bit more. This time, too, he urged me, "*Trink, trink, mein kind*" (Drink, drink, my child).

I drank from the green bottle and smelled the fragrance of tea that it gave off. The drink was warm and sweet.

Suddenly I woke up and shouted, "Where is the man who was standing here?"

The people around me said, "Poor thing. She's gone crazy."

Many times in my life I had dreamed dreams that stirred up tremendous emotions. About two or three weeks before we were taken from our home and sent to the ghetto, I dreamed the strangest dream: I was sitting in our yard in Komjat, when a huge stone suddenly fell from above. My father came and shouted, "Suriko, move aside. The stone is falling on you!" I didn't have time to step aside, but the stone fell alongside me; everyone was killed and only I remained alive. I didn't tell anyone about this dream, but it seemed strange to me and it stayed with me for a long time, throughout my stay in Auschwitz and also during the week of liberation.

I could still taste on my lips the tea that my father had given me in the dream; it was completely real. My father's appearance in the dream was also crystal clear. I had spoken with my father, he had looked me in the eye, and it had seemed to me that he was actually standing next to me. I struggled to accept the fact that it had only been a dream.

During that whole week, people kept taking equipment out of the warehouses: shoes, socks, clothing, dishes, and food. On Thursday I went to the warehouse again, together with a lot of people, and I picked up a clothes brush.

I was debating whether it made any sense to take a clothes brush, since I had no clothes of my own, and anyway, what could one clean with a brush? At that moment I was surrounded by dozens of prisoners who had come to the underground warehouse to look for clothing, shoes, and utensils.

Suddenly a German soldier carrying a rifle came into the warehouse. He yelled in German: "I am a devoted German soldier and I am going to kill you all!" He began to shoot. Screams were heard on all sides. People collapsed; some were wounded and others were dead.

Terrified, I froze in place. I had thought that there were no Germans left in Auschwitz; how could it be that one of them had come back to kill us? How much longer will we continue to be afraid of being killed? When will the moment finally come that we can wake up peacefully in the morning, move about in comfort, and go anywhere we want without worrying that someone is lying in wait to take our lives?

I didn't know any of the prisoners who were in the warehouse at the time. The second I recovered my wits, I ran outside and far, far away from there. When I realized that no one was chasing me and that I could calm down, I stopped and looked down at my hands. I was still clutching the clothes brush that I had been considering when the soldier came in and began mowing people down.

I brought the brush back to the block, put it among my things, and kept it. That brush is still with me, in a drawer by my bed, even though some of its bristles have fallen out over the years.

Among the clothing I took from the warehouses in those days was a garment, like a nightgown, of coarse, blue-gray fabric with thin white stripes. The garment had no sleeves, so I buttoned a shirt over it. It was very wide and the hem reached to below my knees. That garment has also remained with me to this very day. It is displayed in the "Ganzach Kiddush Hashem[29]" in Bnei Brak, a documentation institute for researching and memorializing the Holocaust.

---

29   *Ganzach Kiddush Hashem*: The name of the organization implies that the artifacts from the Holocaust are holy, in the same way that a Torah scroll is holy, because the Jews who died were in fact sanctifying God's name. Please put in parentheses what the name of the organization means (in literal terms).

A Promise from My Grandmother

The weakness and the hunger,
Became so powerful,
That I already lost hope.
All I wanted, my only request,
was a slice of bread.
I remembered my righteous grandmother,
Chana-Devorah, may she rest in peace,
Who would tell me when I was a child,
Quietly and with love,
In Yiddish and the traditional intonation,
From the Torah cantillation,
"He who created the world,
Split the Red Sea,
Brought down manna for forty years in the desert,
Gave the Jews the Torah,
Build the Holy Temple in Jerusalem,
And gave the Jews the Land of Israel as a gift,
He will save us from trouble once again."
He will save a poor girl from Birkenau-Auschwitz.

THE RUSSIANS ARE COMING!

It had been nine days since the Death March set out, leaving us behind in Auschwitz, waiting with bated breath to see who would be victorious: the Germans or the Russians. From time to time we would hear echoes of battles and explosions, but most of the time it was relatively quiet, and we feared that the Russians had lost the battle and the Germans were about to return to Auschwitz.

Before the Sabbath I brought us bread, onions, and potatoes from the warehouses. Some of the sick girls in Block 22 had already gotten out of bed, and a few girls roasted the potatoes over coals. On the Sabbath eve we ate a slice of bread with roasted potatoes topped with onion, a meal such as we had not had for more than 10 months.

On Sabbath morning we awoke to absolute silence. Silence in Auschwitz – an illogical and incomprehensible contradiction. It was the Sabbath of the Torah portion *Beshallach*[30], the Sabbath known as "*Shabbat Shira*" (the Sabbath of Song), after the portion in which the Children of Israel, thousands of years earlier,

---

30   *Torah portion*: Jews read a portion of the Torah publicly in the synagogue every Sabbath morning. The Torah is divided into weekly portions, in an annual cycle, so that each Sabbath is assigned a specific portion.

sang in thanks for the miraculous splitting of the Red Sea when they left Egypt. It was the 13th day of the month of Shvat in the Jewish year 5705 (January 27, 1945).

We got out of bed and looked outside. Auschwitz was covered with fresh snow that had been falling all night. The snow was smooth and even, without a single footstep visible anywhere. For a fraction of a second, the place looked like paradise, but the numbers tattooed on our arms and our run-down physical and emotional states testified to the fact that until a few days earlier, it had been the Gate of Hell.

And we were still in mortal danger. We didn't speak Yiddish among ourselves, or pray aloud, so that those around us wouldn't know that we were Jews. We still feared that someone would try to finish what the Germans had not had the time to do to us.

Towards evening I stood outside the block, hypnotized by the blinding white snow. Suddenly I saw in the distance, three or four blocks away from us, soldiers running towards us. I was sure that they were Germans.

In a panic, I ran to the block to call my friends so we could hide or run away, but a woman standing in the entrance told me, "Don't run, child. Those are the Russians!"

I started to scream, "The Russians are coming!"

Piri and Irene, lying sick on their beds, were alarmed. We were all excited and swept up with emotion. We didn't know whether to rejoice or panic, or if they were really the Russians and whether they had come to save us or kill us.

The Russian soldiers entered our block and as they saw us,

their jaws dropped and their eyes opened wide. They were older and looked to us like "uncles" or "grandfathers." They were not at their best themselves, most of them having being wounded in the long war.

This one was missing a leg, that one an arm, but apparently our condition was worse than theirs. We were emaciated and ill. About a week later I learned that my weight at that time was only 28 kilos.

It seemed to me that the Russians were having difficulty absorbing what had happened in this hellish place. They walked around the block slowly, with careful steps, smiled at us with compassion, and encouraged us in Russian, "Everything will be okay."

Sometimes history designates a person to be in a certain place at a certain time, and thus history designated those Russian soldiers to be our saving angels, the first to arrive at the death camp and reach out a hand of life to the survivors.

The first thing they did was open their packs and pull out preserved food such as sausage, but the Jewish girls politely refused, knowing that the food was not kosher.

Darkness fell, the Sabbath was over, and outside it began to snow again. The snow didn't deter the Russian soldiers, some of whom had not seen their homes in Russia for many months. They decided to organize baths for us. It was obvious that we hadn't showered for weeks, and they heard that we all had lice.

They took three or four large wooden beds out of the block, lit a large bonfire, and placed a giant pot on top. Then they took mattresses and blankets off several beds and created a sort of dry "bridge" from the block entrance to the fire, so that we could go in and out easily. We were not used to such consideration there.

At that stage, there was no electricity in Auschwitz, and the darkness was thick. I heard one of the commanders say to another one in Russian, "Go into town with some of your soldiers and bring back 14 kerosene lamps so there will be light."

The Russian soldier asked, "Where will I get lamps?"

The commander answered, "Go into houses and take them from there."

Half an hour later the soldiers returned with the lamps, and the outdoor "shower" area was bathed in bright light.

They took us out of the block one after the other, instructing us to walk on the mattresses and blankets towards the pot of hot water; they scooped out water in a small pot and washed us while we were still fully dressed, with no soap or disinfectant. They dumped water over my head from a chamber pot, wrapped me in a dry blanket and told me, "Run to the block."

After the shower I lay in bed for about two hours and listened with great excitement to what was happening outside. The light from the lamps shone in through the windows. Many people had arrived at the camp and were walking around outside, speaking loudly and creating a commotion. Among them were older women who introduced themselves as nuns – Polish nuns. There were also local Polish residents who had switched loyalties to be on the side of the victorious Russians, and everyone was making a commotion going in and out of the block.

When it was time to prepare supper, the Russian soldiers shot one of their horses, who had apparently been ill, and passed out portions of raw meat. Outside the block they lit a fire with the boards from a dismantled bed, and then each one took a turn roasting his piece of horse meat.

Holding the chunk of meat I had been given, I went into the block and asked my friends what I should do with it.

Someone asked me quietly, "Do you have some salt so you could salt it and kasher[31] it?"

In some other reality that question could have been amusing – to kasher the non-kosher meat of an impure animal?! But Auschwitz was not a place to seek logic. Auschwitz itself was a place of pure irrationality.

I began to look for salt. Someone said that in the morning they would give us salt, and accordingly I decided to hide my hunk of meat. With a friend, I sought out a secluded corner. We dug a hole in the snow and buried the meat.

I returned to the block and stood outside, leaning on the wall and looking at the people around me. The prisoners included non-Jewish Ukrainians and Communists, who were rejoicing at the coming liberation. Unlike us, they had not lost their families, nor had they experienced tragedy on a national level. We didn't yet know the word "holocaust" and couldn't imagine the scope of the killing, but we knew that the catastrophe we had experienced was not just ours personally, but of the entire

---

31   *kasher*: This refers to one of several steps required to make a piece of meat fit for eating under Jewish law: salting the meat to remove the blood (since Jewish law forbids eating blood). However, as the text points out, this is an absurd consideration in this case, because in the first place the meat must be from a kosher animal (which a horse is not).

Jewish people. There were moments when we thought we might be the only Jews left in the world.

The Ukrainian and Communist women prisoners were kissing and hugging each other, lying down in the snow and singing, crossing themselves, and blessing and thanking the Russians for entering Auschwitz and liberating us. Together with the Russian soldiers they cheered and sang, beside themselves with joy.

Tears filled my eyes and I burst into sobs. I entered the block and went over to my friends, who were still lying in bed with freezing feet, and said, "Where will I go tomorrow, Sunday? Who will be waiting for me? Where will I be? No one is left from my family."

They all joined my weeping, each one worried about her future. None of us had a place to return to. All of us had lost our families.

After a night of weeping and restless sleep, we awoke in the morning to learn that there had been a terrible outbreak of food poisoning. The cause had been the horse meat, which had been infected with bacteria. Anyone who had eaten the meat, and particularly anyone who had eaten it raw, had become terribly ill, and many had breathed their last and lay dead in the snow.

Among the dead were Russian soldiers, Ukrainians, Poles, and Communist prisoners, as well as Jewish prisoners. It turned out that anyone who did not eat the horse meat – was saved.

With heavy hearts, the remaining soldiers and prisoners moved the corpses to other blocks and piled them there. The mass death was a painful contrast to the Gentile prisoners' celebration the previous evening.

SEVENTY YEARS LATER

My mother's story, about looking for salt to *kasher* the piece of horse meat, was a moment of almost comic relief in her story. My father, may he rest in peace, would sit next to us, listen to the story with me, and smile.

"Just imagine," my father would say to me, "Mother went to look for salt to *kasher* unkosher meat from an impure animal!"

My mother would laugh a clear, pleasant laugh. My mother loves to tell jokes and funny stories, and she has a gift for storytelling; since it is her personal story, she has every right to see the salt story as a comic episode. But then my father's gaze would blur and his eyes grow moist, for the story of a young woman in Auschwitz looking for salt to *kasher* horse meat also showed spiritual greatness and a strong, pure, and innocent faith.

"Mother looked for salt to *kasher* the horse meat," my father would say proudly, with admiration, love, and wonder. Even in the depths of Hell, after she had lost her whole family and watched innocent people being slaughtered left and right, Mother tried to continue to observe a Jewish way of life as she had seen in her parents' home. Her faith in the Creator was not eroded under the soldiers' boots, did not dissipate with the sight of the crematorium smoke, and did not disappear in the hunger, exhaustion, or suffering.

The question of faith during and after the Holocaust is fascinating and complex. One day I asked my parents how they could continue believing in the Creator of the World after everything, after all that happened.

"For us it was never even a question," answered my father, who wore a knitted yarmulke[32], served as a synagogue sexton, and set aside time every day for learning Torah. "Mother and I had strong faith in the Creator of the World, and it was clear to us that we wanted to continue to be religious, as our parents were."

I didn't ask again. I was unworthy of even trying to understand how the world is ordered and the meaning of the Creator's "hiding his face" during the Holocaust. The murder during the Holocaust was planned, engineered, and carried out by human beings, with full intent and forethought, just as the atom bomb dropped in that same war was planned, engineered, and carried out by human beings with forethought. On the continuum between the Holocaust and the revival of the Jewish people in their own country, between Auschwitz and the State of Israel, between the totality of the Creator and man's free will, I learned from my parents that in a place where all they have has run out, a simple, inward faith continues to exist.

---

32 Knitted yarmulke (skullcap): In Israel, the type of head covering a man wears indicates the stream of Judaism that he belongs to. A knitted yarmulke generally indicates someone who considers himself part of the religious Zionist movement. The kippot are actually crocheted, and not knitted! It's the same word in Hebrew, however.

During the writing of this book, I took part in the course "Emissaries of Memory" at the Shem Olam[33] Institute; the goal of the course was to provide second-generation Holocaust survivors with tools to document their parents' stories. One of the course participants talked about her father, a survivor of Auschwitz. At the end of her talk she showed on the screen the words of the song "Remember Your Word," based on Psalm 119:49-51: "Remember your word to your servant, for you have given me hope. My comfort in my suffering is this: Your promise preserves my life. The arrogant mock me without restraint, but I do not turn from your law."

As my fellow students, all children of charred remains who had been rescued, hummed along with the melody, I suddenly saw before me the image of my dear parents, singing that song when I was a child. I had not heard it for many years, but melodies that our parents plant in us as children are imprinted on our souls even if we don't hear them for decades. My mother and father loved that song, and sang it with joy and devotion. "The arrogant mock me without restraint, but I do not turn from your law."

The melody of the song was composed towards the end of World War II by Rabbi Eliezer Zusia Portugal, may his memory be for a blessing. He was the founder of the Skulen Hasidic dynasty, originating in Sculeni on the Romanian-Moldavian border. Rabbi Eliezer Zusia spent the end of the war saving orphaned Jewish children. Apparently the song met with success in Eastern Europe even during the war. My mother knew it from her parents' home and remembers her father singing it.

---

33 *Shem Olam*: "Eternal Name."

The song arrived in Israel with the immigrants from Europe, and was beloved by the Israeli national-religious public in the 1950s and 1960s. The terrors of the Holocaust shed new light on the consolation by the author of the Psalms, that the evildoers mocked him but even so he did not abandon God's Torah – that was their consolation, too.

My father also went through difficult things during the Holocaust. Except for one brother, his entire family perished, most of them in Auschwitz. He himself was conscripted into the Hungarian army. After the German occupation, he was taken prisoner, escaped, and wandered the roads for weeks before finally being caught. He was about to be taken out and hung when he managed to escape again and thus was saved. During all that time, among the possessions that he kept were the *tefillin* that he had received before leaving home from his brother Eliezer, of blessed memory ; they are in our possession to this day.

"Even in the most difficult moments in the army, in captivity and while fleeing through the forest," my father said, "there was not a single day that I did not put on tefillin."

"The arrogant mock me without restraint, but I do not turn from Your law."

That is the power of faith of two survivors, who saw everything yet continued to believe in the Creator of the World and to keep his commandments with joy and devotion.

"Just imagine," my father would say in wonder, in admiration. "Mother went to look for salt in order to kasher the nonkosher meat of an impure beast!"

DAYS OF RECOVERY IN AUSCHWITZ

In the midst of all the commotion of burying the dead, on that Sunday morning after the Russians' arrival, we began to fear that now we would be sent on our way and would find ourselves outside Auschwitz, with no home or family to go to. We knew that the train tracks in Poland had been blown up, and we didn't know how we would get back to our hometowns.

But our fears evaporated very quickly. Nurses from the Red Cross arrived, and they explained that we would stay in Auschwitz until we had recovered. They moved us to the other side of the camp, to a place now known as "Auschwitz 1," where the Auschwitz-Birkenau Museum is located.

They housed us in three buildings that had been officers' living quarters. I was placed in the middle of the three buildings. Those buildings were of much better quality than the blocks in Birkenau, and the basement of each had a communal bath house with hot water. Every half hour a different group of liberated prisoners was sent to bathe in the bath house. The nuns rubbed salve on our wounds, cleansed our hair of lice, combed us, cut our fingernails, and took care of us. For the first time in many months we began to look a little like human beings.

My hair, which had been shorn 10 months earlier, had begun

to grow back in Auschwitz, but because of malnutrition and poor hygiene it was short and unkempt, like that of all the other prisoners.

A nurse who examined me asked me to get on the scale. My weight was 28 kilos. Someone said to me that if I had weighed one or two kilos less, I would not have survived.

Three times a day the nuns served us hot, nourishing, cooked meals. Although the food was not kosher, we had to eat it in order to regain our health and strength. Anyone who could get out of bed would come to the table to eat, and those who had difficulty standing up were served their meals in bed.

We had plenty of food to eat there, but even so, each one of us hid bread under her pillow.

The nuns cared for us with great devotion, and every day we got a little stronger. My hair started to regain its former shine, and I gained weight.

One morning, about three weeks after liberation, I woke up with terrible stomach pains. One of the nuns ran to the office and notified the doctors and nurses that I was crying and that I was in pain. Two nurses came, wrapped a blanket around my shoulders, and put me in quarantine. They said to me, "You must have caught typhus."

That whole day I stayed alone in the quarantine room, shivering with cold, suffering from stomach pains, and not knowing what to do. Suddenly I discovered that my dress was spotted with blood. I realized I had gotten my period. When the nun arrived in the quarantine room, bringing me tea, I told her in Polish, "I am not sick with typhus. I got my period."

She ran to call the doctor, and doctors and nurses came running, surrounded my bed, interrogated me, and treated me like a medical miracle. It turned out that during that week, a few other women among the liberated prisoners had also gotten their periods for the first time, after all the months in Auschwitz when they didn't have it, but they had kept it secret. In my case, because I had a stomach ache and was held in quarantine, the medical staff found out, and they thought that I was the first of the prisoners to get a period.

They brought me back to the room and instructed me to stay in bed. Every room had eight beds, lined up in a row, and my bed was in the middle. Doctors and nurses came, poked my abdomen, and said that I had a uterus. They already knew that there were people who had been subjected to medical experiments. Apparently I was fortunate enough to have been miraculously saved from them.

After the doctors left, a tall, stocky nun approached my bed and said, "Yes, you're healthy and you've gotten your period, but you need to know that you will never have children."

I was feeling very low, and therefore I accepted the nun's words quietly, without argument. At that moment it didn't bother me that I would not have children. After all, I didn't have a father, or a mother, or sisters or brothers, or uncles and aunts, or grandparents. What children? Who are those children? What children are you talking about?

After that first time, I didn't get my period again for the three months I spent in the rehabilitation hospital at Auschwitz. I accepted the fact that I would never have children.

One day a strange man came into our room and began brutally beating the girls who lay in the first beds, closest to the door. It turns out that he was a German who had returned to Auschwitz. The girls began screaming, and some of them managed to get out of bed. They ran to call the nuns and the nurses, who came and chased him away.

I understood that we had not yet reached our own place where we could rest. There were still those who wanted to kill us just because we were Jews.

The weeks passed, and they began talking about discharging us from the hospital. One day a man came into our room, the father-in-law of one of the women who was hospitalized with us. She was so overcome with emotion that she fainted and fell to the floor. Alarmed, I screamed for the nuns. They came into the room right away and lifted up the woman. Everyone thanked me for screaming, and I said to them, "Well, at least I got to save someone here . . ."

In my room in the hospital was a young woman named Mayta. Her mother had not been in Auschwitz, but rather had been hidden by Gentiles. After liberation, her mother came to find her, and stayed with us at the hospital.

Mayta's mother said, "When we leave here, they will give us a few sheets and blankets." I didn't understand what she was talking about or why she wanted blankets and sheets. But she was older than us and understood that in the houses we would be returning to, there would be no blankets or sheets waiting for us.

One day, when we were already feeling strong and steady

on our feet, Mayta and I went out, together with seven or eight other girls, and left the hospital to see the town of Oświęcim - Auschwitz

One of the girls led us to the center of the town. We walked through the streets, looking at the shops, and stopped by a candy shop. We saw huge amounts of candy in the shop window – some of them long, like the ones I knew from home, and others shaped like cubes. We pressed our faces to the window and gazed longingly at the beautiful, multi-colored candies. It was a sort of proof that life goes on. There is youth, there is beauty, there is sweetness, there is life.

Each of us excitedly described the candy she knew from her homeland.

"In the Czech Republic we had long candies like that," I said.

"And in Romania we had candies like those . . ." another girl said.

Suddenly the Gentile Polish shop owner came out of his shop, holding a straw broom, and chased us away. He treated us as though we had a contagious disease, as though we were disgusting creatures bothering him, as though he feared that our presence would scare away customers.

We were humiliated. After all, we had done nothing wrong – we had just gotten excited over the candy.

When we returned to the hospital, we told Mayta's mother that the shopkeeper had chased us away while we were look-ing at the candy in the display window. She answered us with the cynicism of an experienced woman schooled in pain, "You should have called an officer or a policeman and reported him as a Communist . . ."

I didn't understand what she was talking about. In those days of liberation from Auschwitz, my self-esteem was so low that I couldn't imagine that a Jewish girl like me could fight a non-Jew and stand up for her herself.

I met Mayta and her mother about a year later in the Land of Israel, in the immigrants' camp in Ra'anana, and our reunion was joyful.

SEVENTY YEARS LATER

At the age of 15 1/2 I turned to my parents during one Shabbat meal and asked to hear everything. Everything!

I had waited a long time to make that request. The Holocaust had already been made clear to me through films, pictures, classes in school, and books. And yet I knew my parents' personal stories only vaguely, only the few details that they had told us up until then.

At that Sabbath meal, I was sitting alone with my parents at the table, since my older sisters were already married.

"I don't know if it's a good idea for me to tell . . ." my mother said, with a questioning glance at my father.

Today I understand them. They didn't want to hurt us. They wanted to raise happy, emotionally strong daughters, a new generation in the Land of Israel, a generation nourished from the safe motherland and not from the terrifying stories of the Holocaust.

My parents began to speak in Yiddish, consulting with each other about whether they should tell me everything. After two sentences they switched to Hungarian, which signaled to me that they really didn't want me to understand their conversation. They had a hierarchy for classifying conversations. When they wanted to include me in their conversation, they spoke Hebrew in my presence. When they wanted me not to understand, they spoke Yiddish. When they wanted to really make sure that I didn't understand – it was in Hungarian.

"Okay," my mother said after they finished their consultation. "Father thinks that it is possible to tell you. You're already a big girl."

"Of course," I said. "I waited until I was the age that you were, Mother, when you were in Auschwitz, 15 1/2. If you went through such terrible things at my age, I can, at the same age, know what you went through."

My parents exchanged glances. I assume that they would rather have told their daughters other stories. But this was the reality of their lives, and they began talking. They told stories during that Sabbath meal, and the next Sabbath, and the next, and the next, and the next . . . and continued talking at a weekday breakfast, at a weekday lunch on another day, and at another weekday dinner, with the bedtime cup of milk, with the four o'clock cup of tea, and with the morning cup of coffee.

The Holocaust stories became part of our way of life. I felt that I had to hear the stories and be a partner to their history. In this way, I felt that I might heal them a little, bring them ease, and relieve their shoulders a little of the heavy burden of painful secrets.

They talked and talked and talked, and I listened and listened and listened. I heard stories about members of my parents' families. Thus I learned that my Aunt Etu (Esther), my father's sister, for whom I am named, together with her sister Gitu, was shot to death in a forest next to the Theresienstadt concentration camp, or possibly died on the Death March, after their release from Auschwitz.

When my sisters came with their families to spend the Sabbath, they would also join in listening to the stories of testimony. When my niece Irit was 12, she also joined us in listening to stories, and, as the third generation, she was one of my mother's most attentive listeners.

My mother became an eyewitness. She was invited to give lectures, and she traveled all over the country – to schools, military bases, workplaces, community centers, and seminaries of Jewish learning.

My parents worked in the diamond polishing business, and in their free time they studied and expanded their horizons. They both loved to study and read. My father was an expert in the world of Torah and my mother specialized in historical and social issues. In their free time outside of work and studies, they both volunteered in various areas. For several decades, under the auspices of the "Emunah" women's charitable organization, my mother volunteered to help run the nationalist-religious women's movement, a "Club for the Older Woman Member," and a Torah college. Twice her activities earned her recognition as a "Beloved of Emunah Organization." In the 1990s, during the large wave of immigration from the Soviet Union, my parents volunteered to help the new immigrants, welcoming them, accompanying them in their absorption into Israel, organizing big ceremonies for *brit milah* (ritual circumcision) in hospitals and for weddings, and accompanying converts in their process of conversion. They lived the message they gave us – that vanquishing the Nazis' acts will come through acts of kindness and increasing good in the world, all with joy and love.

My mother's testimony was recorded and filmed many times. My mother's and father's experiences in the Holocaust were documented, each one separately, as part of the project of the Visual History Foundation, founded by Steven Spielberg at the University of Southern California.

My mother traveled to Poland seven times with youth delegations and, the eighth time, when she was 86, I accompanied her on a trip that she joined as an "eyewitness." The teenagers, who had never met us before, quickly became my mother's grandchildren, and they called her "Grandma Sara," hugged her, and showered her with warmth and love. They eagerly drank in her stories.

"Everywhere that I give eyewitness testimony," my mother told me, "I make sure at the end to bless the audience with all good things. They say that the blessings of a Holocaust survivor have special merit."

Every year on the anniversary of the liberation of Auschwitz, January 27, my father would send my mother flowers, and we would all join in celebrating her day of liberation. My sister Dorit, who was born on January 26, 1951, was given her name from the fact that she was born on the eve of the sixth anniversary of freedom and liberation.[34]

After my father died we continued to mark this day without him, with much longing for him.

---

34 *Dorit*: The name comes from the Hebrew root "dror" meaning liberation, freedom.

My mother continued telling stories and testifying, and the circle of listeners expanded to include the grandchildren and great-grandchildren, third- and fourth- generation survivors.

And one day my mother said to me, "There were things that happened there in Auschwitz that I will never tell . . ."

And I know. And it makes sense.

A TRAIN FROM AUSCHWITZ TO FREEDOM

Spring was coming, and the snow in Auschwitz melted away. One day, going out to the yard to warm myself in the sun, I saw two Jewish men who had just arrived. They addressed me, asking in Hungarian, "Excuse us. Do you know anyone here who speaks Hungarian?"

I said, "Yes, I speak Hungarian also."

They showed me pictures of two gorgeous women wearing beautifully decorated hats, expensive jewels around their necks, and elegant clothing. With tearful eyes and a sob in their voices they asked me, "Did you see these women here? They are our wives. Our paths parted, and we are looking for them, hoping that they are still alive in Auschwitz."

I was amazed at their question. During my time in Auschwitz, hundreds of thousands of Jewish women arrived there. We were all shorn and had lost so much weight that we had become skeletons, so how did they expect me to identify their beautiful wives? I thought to myself that if the women had arrived here with small children, they had most certainly been sent straight to the gas chambers. But I didn't want to say such a hurtful thing to them. The only thing left for me to do was to cry together with them for the loss, the catastrophe.

They asked me, "Where are you from?"

I told them about my birthplace, and they told me that were returning to the city of Satmar, in northern Romania.

I asked, "What's it like in Satmar?"

They said that in those days there were 250 young Jewish men who had been in work camps rather than extermination camps. These men were called *Munkaszolgálat* ("labor force") who were conscripted into the Hungarian army, taken prisoner by the Germans, and continued to work at forced labor in work camps under harsh conditions.

They told me that they had a list of the men's names. I looked through the list with a pounding heart. My mother's older sister, Sheindl of the Gelb family, who was born in Komjat, had lived in Satmar with her husband Levi Yitzhak Leibovits, also from Komjat, and their 10 children. I knew some of the children – Moshe, Meir, and Etu (Esther), who had come to visit us in Komjat a few years earlier. The rest of the children I knew by name only. I had been told that someone had seen Moshe and Meir Leibovits, who had been in Auschwitz and then sent to the Warsaw Ghetto to help remove the rubble after the uprising there.

My eyes darted over the list with great tension and excitement, and lo and behold: I found the name Shalom Leibovits.

"Shalom Leibovits!" I cried excitedly, my eyes flooding with tears. "He's my cousin! He's alive!"

I burst into sobs, barely able to speak. I had never met Shalom, who was seven years older than me. I asked, "What's he like?"

"He's a nice guy," they both responded, "friendly and

welcoming, well-behaved, solid, good-looking, 24 years old, a hard worker. To make a living, he opened a shoemaking workshop."

I rejoiced to hear that my cousin was still alive, but since I had never met him, and because he was older than me, and from a different country, I didn't think about contacting him.

The holiday of Passover passed, the month of April 1945 arrived, and they began discharging us from the hospital in Auschwitz. Each time they discharged a group of men and women together. The first to leave were the ones who lived in Poland, because it was already possible to travel within the country. They gave them a note from the Red Cross, stating that they had been prisoners in a camp, and that they should be given free train rides, as well as food and drink at the distribution points.

My turn came to be discharged from the hospital. With great excitement, I packed three dresses that had been given me in Auschwitz, together with my other meager belongings. I boarded a train going to Slovakia and from there to the Czech Republic, to Yugoslavia, to the Carpathian Mountains, and to Hungary. In each car they seated men and women from the same country. There were hundreds of people on that particular train journey.

I looked around at the other travelers in the car, some of whom I had met in Auschwitz, and discovered that I was the only one from our village, Komjat. There was someone from Salish, the village close to ours where I had begun my junior high school studies. But I had lost contact with everyone that I knew from Komjat who had been with me at the beginning, in

Lager A in Auschwitz. Everyone had scattered. We had entered Auschwitz together, and then every one had her own experiences after that.

During the war, train tracks in Poland had been blown up, and there were stretches of our journey in which we had to get out of the train, take a ferry across a river, and continue the trip on another train.

During the trip I looked out the window at the sprawling landscapes we passed by. Spring was bursting out everywhere, as though Europe had not just gone through a bloody war. We traveled during the day, and the train stopped in a city each night. When we reached Krakow, together with a few other girls I had met on the train, I walked to Daluga Street, where there had been a Jewish welfare assistance office. When we arrived there, everything had been broken into and smashed. We hung a blanket in place of a door and slept there. The next morning we boarded another train and rode to Slovakia. From there we took another train to Debrecen and from there to Prague. The bridge over the Borzhova River had been destroyed, so on Friday they took us across the river on a small ferry that held 10 people. On the other side of the river we boarded a train going to Salish.

I arrived in Salish on Friday evening. There I found many Jews who had hidden out during the war and never got to the camps. They had not even heard of the Death March. They began to interrogate me and asked me to tell them what I had been through.

They told me that I would be sleeping in a room with two

girls, but the guard came in and slept in the same room. I felt terrible. I didn't sleep a wink the whole Sabbath. We slept in an abandoned house whose Jewish owners had not returned from the camps. Windows and doors had been stolen from the house, but they fixed it up for those returning from the camps. I felt that I couldn't spend another night in that house.

Early on Sabbath afternoon I decided to walk to Komjat. I left my backpack in Salish and took only a small bag with me. The two girls in the house promised to watch over the bag.

I crossed the familiar fields on the way to my village. To my home. A year earlier I had left here with my parents and five siblings, and now I was returning here alone. A charred branch rescued from the fire, the only survivor of the whole family.

I entered Komjat and began walking through the streets of the village. Suddenly someone called to me, "Suri Hershkovits!" He ran towards me, sobbing.

I saw that it was Yoel, who was five years younger than my father and had a wife, Esther, and five children, one of whom had been a classmate of my brother's. At first I didn't recognize him, for he was without a beard or sidecurls. Through his tears, he told me that his wife and five children had perished in Auschwitz.

"Komjat is not like it was when you left it," he told me sorrowfully. "The sky has fallen. There are no observant Jews, no synagogue, no kosher food. Everyone is sleeping with everyone else and if you want to stay and sleep at my place, you can."

I was shocked. Me? Sleep at a man's house? I refused his offer.

I wandered the streets of our village with tearful eyes. I

discovered that very few Jews had returned to Komjat. I came to my parents' home, our big, beautiful house, and discovered that the municipality had taken over half of it, since a bomb had fallen on the town hall at the end of the war. One room facing the field housed a non-Jewish family.

The door to our house was open, like a municipality office, and people were going in and out. I went inside. The house looked completely different; it had been turned into an office. They had set up a bookshelf of documents in the living room.

The clerks, recognizing me, got out of their seats and came up to me. They told me, "You can live in the room where your grandmother used to live."

I glanced at the little room where Grandma Chana-Devorah had lived. It looked like a storeroom, full of crates of documents. I refused their offer. I didn't want to live alone in a place where non-Jews were going in and out. I left the house, shocked and broken. The clerks followed me out and gave me a box containing seven silver spoons that had belonged to our family. They thought it was a way to placate me. I took the spoons. They were the only things left from my family and my home, but they offered neither appeasement nor comfort.

In the house opposite the empty synagogue, I discovered Hinda Weissman of the Leibovits family, the seamstress who had taught me to sew, and who had been with me in the first weeks in Auschwitz. Her husband had not returned, and the infant whom she had borne in camp, on account of whom she had been taken to Germany, had been murdered.

Hinda said to me, "Come, stay and live with me." I stayed

at Hinda's for a few days, but we were very crowded there, for other girls from the village were also living there, girls who didn't have houses to return to. We slept three girls to a bed.

The first evening a few Jews, who had hidden out in the forest and now returned to the village, came and asked to hear what we had gone through. They knew that it had been terrible in the camps, but didn't know everything. When we told them, their eyes widened in shock and they asked, again and again, "Really?"

We talked until late into the night about what we had been through in Auschwitz, and all of us were crying.

Later that night, when everyone had left, one of the young men, Srul Weiss, came up to me and told me, "I have *yahrzeit*[35] this week and there is no *minyan* here in Komjat. I'm really ashamed of that. So on Wednesday I'm going to Satmar, where there are lots of Jews and there is a *minyan*. Do you know that you have a cousin in Satmar? Shalom Leibovits, he's my second cousin."

I told him I knew.

Srul asked if I wanted to write something to Shalom. I agreed and wrote a note. He left on Wednesday morning for Satmar, and that evening he found Shalom at the afternoon prayer service and gave him the note.

Shalom read the note, and on Thursday morning he dropped everything and set out on the torturous journey from Romania to Komjat.

---

35   *yahrzeit*: Yiddish for "anniversary," the anniversary of someone's death. On the yahrzeit, children of the deceased recite the mourner's prayer, which can only be said in a *minyan* (a prayer quorum of at least 10 men).

On Friday, a minute before the Sabbath began, I stood on a small bridge at the entrance to Hinda Weissman's house and watched a group of young men and women who had just come from the train station to the village. They included people who were returning to the village after the camps, and I wanted to see who was coming. A few meters away from me stood a young man whom I did not know, and someone pointed to me and told him, "Here, this is Suri."

The young man approached me, smiling, and introduced himself, "Shuli Leibovits, your cousin, son of Sheindel, your mother's sister. I think I am also the only one remaining from my whole family. We were 10 children, but no one is left except me."

Later we found out that one of Shalom's brothers, Moshe Arieli, who was sent from Auschwitz to clear away the rubble after the Warsaw Ghetto uprising in Poland, had escaped, joined the Polish Resistance in Warsaw, spent time in a POW camp, and eventually immigrated to Israel. Shalom and Moshe were the only ones who survived out of their whole family, but at the time we didn't know that.

Shalom and I embraced and burst into sobs on each other's shoulders.

That Sabbath, Shalom stayed with a friend in the village. It was a very emotional Sabbath for us. People were reunited after many months, and each one was recounting what he or she had been through. Shalom told us that many Jews returning from the camps lived in Satmar. He suggested that I come live in Satmar, too.

After the Sabbath I decided to accept his offer. I realized that

I had no reason to stay in a place where my family no longer existed and I couldn't move back into my own house. I packed up my paltry belongings and walked with Shalom to Salish to pick up my backpack. From there we walked back to my house in Komjat. We went to the cowshed and looked for the pit where my mother had hidden the parcel before we were taken from our home. I found a pit with a metal box inside it. The cover was broken, and there was little left of the original parcel other than a few embroidered napkins, which I took with me. All my worldly possessions now consisted of my backpack, together with a blanket that had been given to me, which I tied to the outside of the pack.

The next evening I went with friends from our village to the Czech Embassy in Bucharest. Like the rest of the group, I wanted to get a Czech passport, since I couldn't travel around without a passport. Shalom boarded the train with us but got out in Satmar, carrying my backpack. My friends and I continued on the night train.

I stayed in Bucharest for a week, sleeping at a hotel organized by the Czech Consulate. On Thursday night, passports in hand, we got back on the train, heading north again. We rode the train all that night and the next day, and it seemed to me to be moving far too slowly. When I saw that the sun was about to set, I worried that I would still be on the train on the Sabbath,[36] but then it stopped and the conductor called out, "Satmar!"

---

36   *on the train on the Sabbath*: Observant Jews do not travel on the Sabbath, so they need to arrive at their destination before sundown on Friday evening.

I got out on the platform in Satmar, Romania; it was my first time in the city. I asked people to direct me to the street where Shalom lived with a friend, next to the Jewish ghetto, and reached his house a minute before the Sabbath began. Shalom had already left for the synagogue, but I went in and lit Sabbath candles.

The cycle of a week had come to a close, and I closed my eyes and welcomed the Sabbath in breathless anticipation of new beginnings.

That week, the Jewish hospital in Satmar had opened rooms for Holocaust survivors who had returned home, and I was given a bed in a room with 10 other girls. As a symbolic contribution towards maintaining the place, we worked shelling nuts. They brought us a big sack of nuts, and we sat and shelled them by hand.

Shalom came to visit me every day. Once he brought me a roll, and another time some cake. He took me to see the shoe-maker's shop that he had opened with two friends, and showed me the city.

One day we were sitting, talking about the past and the future, and we were both crying. Shalom told me that he made a good living and then asked gently, "We're going to get married, right?"

I started to cry again. I told him that the nun in the hospital in Auschwitz had told me that I would never have children. It hurt me to think that not only had I suffered so much up until now, but that even in the future I would not be a normal person. I couldn't accept the fact that the Nazis had cut off my past, ruined my present, and destroyed my future as well.

Shalom immediately said, "Oh, she just wanted to scare you. We have *a groyse Gott* (a great God) and we will have children."

We got up and went to Rabbi Weiss, the rabbi of the Satmar yeshiva, and told him that we had decided to get married. In great excitement, the rabbi warmly congratulated us and arranged with us for the wedding to take place the following week.

We went to check the house where Shalom's parents, Sheindel and Levi Yitzhak Leibovits, had lived with their 10 children. They lived at 18 Cuza Voda Street, around a courtyard housing the offices of *Hapoel Hamizrachi*[37] of Satmar, which Levi Yitzhak had directed. There was a synagogue there with a social hall, but everything was empty, neglected, dirty, and broken.

We began cleaning up the room looking out on the main street. A friend came and helped us clean. We brought windows from houses that still had unbroken windows, and little by little the place began to look like a home.

---

37 *Hapoel Hamizrachi*: A religious Zionist organization that supported the establishment of agricultural settlements in Israel where work was done according to Jewish law.

SEVENTY YEARS LATER

I had always wanted to see the village where my mother was born, Komjat.

She herself had not been there for 67 years, since she discovered that the municipality staff had invaded her house and taken it over for themselves.

Three years ago we organized a small family expedition and set out, seven family members, together with my mother. First we sought out my father's house in Satmar, Romania, and then my mother's house in the village now called Veliki Komyati and located in the Ukraine.

First we came to Satmar. Today it is home to a small Jewish community, a far cry from the large community that thrived there in the past. At number 18 on a street now named Leon Cuza Voda we found the Leibovits home, now occupied by Romanian residents. The room that had served as the offices of Hapoel Hamizrachi was empty and abandoned.

The residents of the house welcomed us and offered us apricots from the tree, one of the fruit trees that my mother remembers as being in the yard 70 years earlier.

"There was a walnut tree here," my mother recounted. "When the Leibovits children were little, enterprising Moshe would get up first in the morning, climb the tree, and pick nuts before anyone else. And here was the little garden that I cared for," she said, pointing to the dirt yard.

At the end of the visit to the house and yard, we asked my mother if she remembered the location of the shoemaker's workshop that belonged to my father, of blessed memory.

"Of course," my mother responded. "I would bring him his lunch every day."

My mother set off through the streets of Satmar with us trailing behind. She turned into a side street, stopped in front of a shop, and announced, "This was Shalom's workshop!"

To our amazement, there was a modern shoe shop in the same location.

We entered the shop with pounding hearts and looked at the shelves crowded with shoes. My mother gazed wide-eyed at the sewing machine.

"Yes, of course," my mother concluded. "That's the sewing machine that I used to sew our sheets and towels!"

It was strange and exciting to reach the village of Komjat, of which we had heard so much. The village is planted among breathtaking vistas of the Carpathian Mountains, and it was as though it had frozen in place since the years it was under Soviet rule. There are no stairways in the village, the roads are cracked, and the residents are simple peasants.

"The place looks much worse than it did when we lived here," my mother observed, eyes wide with sorrow and amazement as she looked around.

Today there is not a single Jew in this village or in the nearby villages.

We were excited to find the remains of the Jewish house of study of the village, which had stood next to the large synagogue, of which there was now no trace. We found, to our great dismay, that the house of study, displaying a Star of David, was now dirty and served as a warehouse.

In the Jewish cemetery we found the grave of Grandma Chana-Devora, which had been restored a few years earlier by her grandchildren and great-grandchildren, members of the Rozenberg family, originally from the Gelb family, who live in the United States. How our eyes sparkled as we stood before Grandma's grave! For the first time in our lives we were at Grandma's grave! For me, standing next to her grave was the closest I had ever come in my life to a feeling of "Grandma."

We read chapters of Psalms and held the memorial ceremony for her that we had never been able to have.

We left the street where the cemetery was located and searched for my mother's house. Time blurs many things and causes them to be forgotten, but my mother knew exactly where her family's house should be standing. We were looking forward to seeing the house, going inside, and hearing my mother's stories about it, about her parents and little brothers and sisters, but to our great disappointment, it turned out that the building had been razed several years earlier and a large supermarket now stood in its place. Perhaps it was a remnant of the same grocery shop that Grandma Chana-Devorah ran here, and after her my mother's father – the shop that was expropriated from our family during the war and given to the non-Jewish neighbors.

We stood before the expanse of the plot of land that had

belonged to the Gelb family and then the Hershkovits family.

"We had grapevines," my mother recounted, "and we had corn and wheat fields. But this place was not ours. Our place is in the Land of Israel. That is where our home is."

As part of the journey back to our family roots, we traveled with my mother to Auschwitz.

"Grandma, what should we wear tomorrow for our visit to Auschwitz?" asked one of my mother's grandchildren.

We were all asking ourselves the same question. I understood why young people entered Auschwitz wrapped in Israeli flags – perhaps to give themselves extra confidence and pride.

"What do you mean?" my mother responded. "We'll dress as nicely as possible. We are returning to Auschwitz as victors!"

And so it was. And yet, as we stood at the entrance to Auschwitz-Birkenau, our eyes following the train tracks stretched out before us, running under the curved entrance gate to the camp, our breath caught in our throats. A shiver of fear ran through me. We had arrived at Hell on Earth, the place built by the children of the Devil, the place that I had feared my whole life.

With dread and trepidation we passed under the gate with my mother. Fear paralyzed us, second- and third-generation survivors. It was our first visit to Auschwitz. My mother, her five grandchildren, and I linked arms to give each other strength.

"Before we go in, I want to tell a joke," said my mother, the girl from Auschwitz who had returned to the camp with her descendants.

For a moment I looked at her open-mouthed, but

immediately recovered my composure. Proudly and coura-geously, my mother told a joke about a *yeshiva* student who asked his rabbi for advice on finding a suitable wife. And thus, in the small act of telling a joke at the entrance to the most horrifying place in the world, my mother taught us all that this is what life is like – sadness alongside laughter, mourning alongside joy – and one must know how to take charge of them and bring them into your life in the proper doses, so as not to become submerged on either side. We laughed at my mother's joke and at the same time wiped away the tears that ran down our cheeks as we laughed.

Thus we entered Auschwitz-Birkenau.

We walked along the train tracks, passed the "ramp" where the passengers had alighted from the trains, and stopped along-side the single car that is now placed next to the tracks as a symbol. We went into Birkenau and stopped next to the ruins of the crematorium. Here, or in the adjacent crematorium, was the workplace of Grandpa Yakov Hershkovits, may God avenge his blood, an honest, righteous, pure man, who was forced to perform the hardest, most back-breaking labor in Auschwitz: to drag corpses and burn them in a fire. In the months when my grandfather worked here, many members of his family arrived in Auschwitz from the Carpathian region, at that time part of Hungary. I am horrified at the thought that my grandfather may have seen his aunts, uncles, and cousins among the dead. That is an unbearably painful thought.

Next to the remains of the crematorium I did something that I had wanted to do for many years but never dared; I leaned over and kissed the number tattooed on my mother's arm, A-7807.

You are no longer a number, I wanted to tell her, and we, who have returned here with you, are proof of that.

With my mother we went into Block 20, which had remained undamaged. My mother led us between the beds and showed us where her board had been located in Block 16, of which only a fragment of the stove in the center of the block remained.

"I slept on this board with 13 other girls," my mother said, pointing to the upper bunk on the left side, in the left inner quarter of the block.

"Grandma, can I climb up to the board?" asked one of the granddaughters, red-eyed. "To feel what you felt there, on the bed?"

"No," my mother said with a smile. "Of course not. Come home with me. There you'll find my real bed, with a clean sheet, smelling freshly laundered."

We all burst into heart-rending sobs.

When we left Auschwitz-Birkenau, we stood in the entrance and gazed at the camp. My daughter, who was then 17, looked sadly at the bunkers.

"Why are you sad?" asked my mother, giving her granddaughter a hug. "We won. Don't you understand? There's a good ending. We established a state. We have a home in the Land of Israel."

Leaving Auschwitz, our driver pulled into a gas station, and in the meantime we spotted a freezer full of popsicles standing outside the station shop. Peeking in the freezer, we discovered ice cream with a label sold in Israel. Suddenly we craved something sweet, to make up for the anguish that our souls had undergone in the wake of the difficult stories and sights that we had heard and experienced up until then. We called a rabbi in Israel and asked him to check for us the kosher status of that brand, which we so longed for. The rabbi asked us to call back in a few minutes.

"To tell the truth, I don't know if I can eat anything now, particularly here," someone from the family said quietly.

We all exchanged glances. We felt like she did; we couldn't eat anything. Even if the soul wanted to sweeten the bitterness for itself, the body could not do it. We got in the car and drove away. The driver asked when we wanted to stop to eat, since we had not eaten lunch yet and it was almost evening. We asked him to drive as far away as possible from there, as far away as possible from Auschwitz.

NEW LIFE AND NEW BEGINNINGS IN SATMAR

My wedding to Shalom took place in the month of Sivan in the Jewish year 5705 (June 1945). Someone lent Shalom a suit and tie, and someone else lent me a white blouse, a long white skirt, and a bridal veil. We decorated the skirt with green leaves.

Piri, a Jewish neighbor who lived opposite us, offered to hold the wedding in her yard, since her yard was larger than ours. On the morning of the wedding, while I was still sewing, altering the skirt and blouse to fit my thin figure, several young men came into our yard, dragging a large box containing beer for the wedding. I was shocked, but they said, "We'll do anything for Shuli."

Indeed, people I had never met came to the wedding. Everyone brought food, and they danced and celebrated with us. Jews whom I did not know, passing by on the street and seeing a wedding, came in to join our festivities.

When they photographed us after the wedding ceremony, they placed a stone in front of me and told me to stand on it, to make me look taller than I really was. Later, when we emigrated to Israel and were taken to Cyprus by the British, they confiscated our belongings, including the photographs we had with us, and among them the wedding picture. Fortunately, while still in Satmar I remembered by heart the addresses of my two uncles who had emigrated to the Land of Israel before the war. After the wedding we sent them the picture by mail, from Romania to Israel. When we ourselves arrived in Israel, they brought us the wedding picture, and thus it is in my possession today.

We fixed up the apartment nicely. Shalom bought fabric for bedding, and in a single day I learned how to sew on the industrial sewing machine in his shoemaking workshop, and that same day I made us sheets. Shalom brought terrycloth fabric, and I cut out and sewed face and hand towels, and even added embroidery for beauty and charm. I was not yet 17 years old, and I was already a "*balabusta*."[38] We were newlyweds and very happy.

Around Passover time we all gathered in the large synagogue in Satmar for a special funeral ceremony for the "*R.J.F.*"[39] soap that many of us had collected and brought from Auschwitz, having been told that they were made from the fat of Jews, in order to eventually bring them to burial. As I gathered the bars of soap in a kerchief, I buried a note among them on which I

---

38 *balabusta*: Yiddish for "housewife," literally "mistress of the house,"

39 *R.J.F.*: An acronym for *reine* (clean), *judische* (Jewish), *fett* (fat). As noted earlier, scholars now believe that these were only rumors, and that human fat was never used commercially to make soap during the Holocaust. The soap bars in Auschwitz were also imprinted with the letters RIF, which can be mistaken for RJF, and this helped feed the rumors. However, during the Holocaust, there were Jews who believed the rumors, and a number of such ceremonies were conducted after the war to bury the bars of soap.

wrote that I did not know from whom this fat had been taken and whom they had used to make the soap, because it could have been from any of us, and if they reached my parents, my sisters, my brothers, and the rest of my family, they should tell them that I had gathered up the remains of whoever they were. We sat in the synagogue, studied *Mishnayot*,[40] read Psalms, cried, and walked together in a procession to the cemetery, where we buried the bars of soap in the earth.

The fast day of the 17th of Tammuz[41] arrived, which is also Shalom's birthday, and I began to cry, remembering that a year earlier I had still been in the camp. That day in Auschwitz had been particularly hard; it was a hot day, we were filthy, and some people had committed suicide and we had seen them left lying against the electric fence. Shalom soothed me, begging me not to fast, and I recovered and came back to myself.

A week passed, and I began vomiting. I could only eat bread with butter and drink milk. Every day I cooked lunch and brought it to Shalom at his workshop, but I myself couldn't look at the food. Shalom was concerned that I had stomach problems.

On Tisha b'Av I was very ill. A Jewish doctor lived across from our house, and I decided to go to him. The doctor was happy to see Shalom. He was a religious man, and before he was taken to the camp, he used to pray and read from the Torah in the synagogue where Shalom prayed. His wife and children had

---

40 *Mishnayot* (singular: Mishna – from the root "study by repetition"): Part of the Jewish oral law, written down in the third century C.E.

41 17th of Tammuz : A Jewish fast day commemorating the breaching of the walls of Jerusalem before the destruction of the Second Temple.

all perished in Auschwitz, and he was left by himself.

The doctor embraced Shalom and cried. He asked how old I was, and I answered that I was 17. The doctor hit his head painfully. "My daughter would have been 17 now," he said.

We all grieved greatly. Then we told him that I was vomiting every morning.

He asked, "And what do you do after that?"

I said, "At ten I eat bread and butter, but I can't eat any other foods."

The doctor's face lit up with a big smile. He clapped Shalom on the shoulder and praised him. I didn't understand. A minute ago we had all been sad, so why was the doctor suddenly so happy? I couldn't stand the doctor being happy while I was suffering.

I asked, "Doctor, have you heard of such a thing – stomach pains that then go away?"

He answered, "Of course. Nine months."

Shalom and I almost fainted. After the doctor checked me we went back home, not knowing whether to rejoice or be sad. We were happy that we would become parents, but we had no grandparents, no parents, and no siblings with whom to share our joy.

Passover Eve in the Jewish year 5706 (1946) arrived, and on the same evening when Jews throughout the world were celebrating the Exodus from slavery to freedom, our oldest daughter, Dalia, was born. She was a beautiful, enchanting baby. A marvel. We were over the moon with excitement, unable to believe that we had merited such a special miracle. Two Holocaust survivors holding in their arms their daughter, the continuity of life. We were so happy. We wanted to name her after our two mothers – Sheindel and Blima. "Sheindel" means "beautiful," and "Blima" means "flower," We looked for the name of a flower in Hebrew, and thus called our daughter Dalia-Yaffa,[42]

When Dalia was a month old, thieves came in through the window one night and stole everything we owned, including our *ketubah* (marriage contract). Although the war was already long over, crime had not ceased to exist in the world.

Shalom continued working with his two partners in the shoemaker's workshop. One of them was a shoemaker, and he prepared the first stage of the shoe. Shalom continued with the second stage, cutting the leather and attaching it to the shoe. The third partner was responsible for the last stage, sewing the shoe on the machine. The shop was located on a main street, and many people came in and bought shoes from them. I also had the privilege of having them make me several beautiful pairs of shoes.

I worked the garden next to our house and planted flowers and vegetables there. One day I went out to the yard with baby Dalia. I spread out a blanket under the cherry tree which, not yet recovered from the war, had yet to bear fruit, lay the baby on the blanket and sat down beside her. We were both enjoying the pleasant sunshine. Suddenly two young men came into the courtyard, introducing themselves as counselors in the *Bnei Akiva*[43] youth movement in Romania. They said they wanted

---

42 In Hebrew, "Dalia" is the flower "dahlia," and "Yaffa" means "beautiful,"

43 Bnei Akiva: At that time (1946) the youth wing of the "Hapoel Hamizrachi" Movement.

to bring people to our courtyard to clean the synagogue and the study hall, which belonged to Hapoel Hamizrachi.

As soon as they left, I took the baby carriage and ran with Dalia to tell Shalom.

He responded, "Thank God!" He was happy that the branch of Hapoel Hamizrachi would be revived and would continue operating from our courtyard, as it had been under his father's direction.

In the following weeks the young men began cleaning and renovating the place. First a Hapoel Hamizrachi synagogue was opened, where ultra-Orthodox Jews with sidecurls prayed and learned Torah alongside Jews who had given up their sidecurls after the Holocaust and grown out the hair on their head, like Shalom.

Later a man named Mark came to the courtyard. Mark had been appointed by Bnei Akiva to direct the training that was going to be held in the courtyard. He introduced himself and told us that he had been a Zionist even before the war. He was followed by about 30 young women and 30 young men, who had signed up for training in preparation for emigration to the Land of Israel. We also joined them and became part of a *gar'in*[44] for a "Torah v'Avoda"[45] kibbutz.

Together we lived a communal kibbutz life. The girls lived in

44 *gar'in* ("seed"): A small group of people who join together to found new settlements (in Israel).

45 "*Torah v'Avodah*" ("Torah and Work"): The motto of the Bnei Akiva movement. A Torah v'Avodah kibbutz is one that belongs to the religious kibbutz movement.

one building, in a few rooms, and the boys in another building. Shalom and I continued living in the room where we had been living before, and a few other married couples were also given individual rooms. At that time we were the only couple who already had a child, and she became the baby of the gar'in. Since we had added the title "*Hachaver*" or "*Hachavera*"[46] to each other's names, when Dalia learned to talk, she called Shalom "*Hachaver Tati* (Daddy)." On the Sabbath, when Shalom would bless the wine, we sometimes had dozens of single men and women around us. Although I was younger than they were, I was considered mature and experienced because I was married with a child.

Among the members of the training group was a 13-year-old, Meli Leibovits, from a village in the Marmarosh region of the Carpathian Mountains, a survivor of Auschwitz and the only one left of his family. Shalom took the orphan boy under his wing and became close to him, partially because of the identical last name, Leibovits. He taught Meli to put on *tefillin* and pray, and taught him Hebrew and the weekly Torah portion. Meli was a handsome, likable boy. Little Dalia adored him. He would sit with us in the dining hall on the Sabbath, and soon became part of our little family. After we emigrated to Israel, we sent him to study at *Mikveh Yisrael*,[47] and, to our great sorrow, when he was 15 he went out into the fields at the agricultural school, stepped on a mine, and was killed. We felt as though we had lost a son. I don't remember whether his full name was

---

46   *Hachaver/Hachavera*: Male/female form of the word meaning "Comrade."

47   *Mikveh Israel* ("The Hope of Israel"): A youth village and agricultural boarding school in central Israel.

Mendel or Shmuel; I only remember his nickname, Meli. May his memory be for a blessing.

During the training, all our housekeeping was communal. Everyone worked and contributed their salaries to the kibbutz. Some of us worked in a wine shop and others in a furniture shop. We cooked together in the kitchen and ate together in the dining hall. Since I was taking care of the baby, I didn't go out to work, but instead helped with secretarial work and in the kitchen, always with Dalia in her carriage at my side.

Every day they trained us in preparation for emigration to Israel: We had classes on the Land of Israel, we learned about various places in the country, we learned to speak Hebrew, and we sang songs in Hebrew. We all trembled with joy at the opportunity we were given to emigrate to the Land of Israel. Occasionally Zionist leaders would come to visit us, and they would make enthusiastic speeches and recount stories of the Land of Israel with glowing eyes.

EMIGRATION TO THE LAND OF ISRAEL

It was a year and a half since Dalia was born. The High Holy Days of the Jewish year of 5708, autumn 1947, arrived, and we were still in Satmar and members of the "Torah v'Avodah" training *gar'in*. We were waiting eagerly for the moment when we could emigrate to the Land of Israel with the gar'in.

For the holidays I cooked the dishes that I remembered from my parents' home and baked the same honey cookies that my mother and grandmother used to bake. I still bake those cookies today, and they are favorites of my children, grandchildren, and great-grandchildren.

Two days after the Jewish New Year, Shalom went out to buy a third machine for his workshop from a Jew who was emigrating to the Land of Israel. I went with him to see the machine, and after we agreed to purchase it, I went back home with Dalia.

When I entered the courtyard, I saw that there was some kind of bustle in the air. Men and women ran up to me, asking, "Where were you? We're waiting for you! Tonight at midnight we're leaving on a bus to Bucharest, and from there to a ship headed for the Land of Israel!"

My heart pounded with excitement. "Tonight?"

The comrades told me that the plan was to travel in a bus

belonging to a Jewish resident of Satmar. He would park the bus on a street in Bucharest and come with us to the ship that was waiting in Bulgaria. They said that everything was being done secretly so that the Gentile neighbors wouldn't find out that we were sailing for the Land of Israel, lest we get arrested. They told the Gentile man who maintained our courtyard that we were going to another city to watch a soccer game.

I ran with the baby carriage to Shalom, hoping to stop his purchase of the machine, but I didn't find him. I came back home, and just then he returned. I told him that we were leaving that night and that we had to get ready for the journey. Even though it sounded like a dream, Shalom immediately declared, "Oh, the Messiah has come!" And indeed, emigrating to Israel for us was like the arrival of the Messiah.

We packed our scanty possessions into a backpack and, with great expectation, I packed the challahs and honey cookies left from the New Year holiday. Suddenly, I remembered that Shalom had only one pair of socks. I ran to Shalom's cousin who lived in Satmar to ask him for another pair of socks.

We left on Thursday and set out for Bucharest by bus with all the gar'in members. We dozed during the long trip, suddenly waking up to find that the bus had stopped. It turned out that it had broken down. The driver decided to take it to the neighboring village for repairs. We all got out onto the road, but we couldn't stand on the roadside, and we didn't know if the bus would in fact be fixed, so we started walking. Shalom and I were carrying our backpack and Dalia in our arms.

The sun rose, and after some time the bus caught up to us.

We boarded it and continued the journey. Towards the Sabbath we reached a village that was near the road, where we stopped to get ready for the Sabbath. When it was over, at midnight on Saturday night, we boarded the train to Bucharest. There were hundreds of people at the train station, and there was a great commotion boarding the train. We feared that there might not be room for all of us, and the members of our gar'in climbed onto the train through the windows. Shalom got in through the window first. I handed him Dalia and the parcels, and then people helped me climb through the window myself.

Everyone around us was excited about moving to Israel, but there were also ugly stories about people who tried to buy other people's places. We had three travel permits that we had bought in Satmar with our own money. Someone approached us and proposed that we leave the baby in Romania and sell him her travel permit. Shalom, furious, sent him away.

When we got out of the train in Bucharest, Jews of that city welcomed us with food and drink. That night we slept around the train station, waiting to board the next train. Again the next morning there was a great uproar in boarding the trains. We ran to one, but it was full; we ran to another one, and when we had already managed to board it, we found that all the seats were taken. We had no choice but to sit on the floor.

We got as far as a kilometer from the Romanian-Bulgarian border, which followed the Danube River. All the trains came to a halt, and they opened the doors of one train at a time, taking out all the passengers, and transferring them to a ferry waiting to cross the Danube.

We sat in the train for a long time, waiting for our turn.

Finally Shalom said to me, "Wait here with the baby. I'm going to find out why it's taking so long."

When he returned, he told me that they were not checking people's travel permits at all, but just transferring people and counting them at the entrance to the ferry. People without permits were also going through, so it was possible that the spots on the ferry could run out. He proposed that we go and stand in the line to board the ferry.

We got out of the train, ran to the ferry, and managed to board it. Ten minutes after we got on, they closed the transit point, and all those who had not gotten on, including those who had paid for tickets to Israel, remained behind in Romania. Those people had to wait several weeks for the next boats.

We stood on the ferry, some 5,000 people, and we all sang together with one heart, "As long as in the heart within . . ."[48] with tears streaming down our faces. I don't think that there was a single dry-eyed person.

From that moment on we could relax, for we knew that anyone who crossed the Danube would board the ship.

After leaving the ferry, we walked for a long time and slept outdoors until we reached the next train. We boarded it on the eve of Yom Kippur (the Day of Atonement), and there we were given honey, jam, canned milk, and challahs.

Close to the start of Yom Kippur, the train stopped part-way

---

48 The opening words of the first stanza of *Hatikvah* (The Hope), a poem by Naftali Herz Imber, which became – and is until this day – the national anthem of the State of Israel.

through its journey, in the midst of Bulgarian fields. We could see nothing but agricultural land in every direction. We got out of the train and prepared to usher in the holy day. The men pulled out tallitot and prayerbooks, and we all stood for the "*Kol Nidre*"[49] prayer. That was one of the most emotional prayers in my life. Yom Kippur in a field, en route to the Land of Israel! I remember looking at Shalom, who was praying with his tallit over his head. We all felt the footsteps of the Messiah.

On Yom Kippur afternoon baby Dalia began vomiting, shaking, and burning up with fever. I walked among the hundreds of people, looking for a doctor. I found one who gave her a spoonful of medicine, and her condition improved.

The doctor said to me, "Look, there, in the distance, there's a house. Go and ask the tenants for a cup of milk. It will help the baby." I went to that house and gave them my sweater in exchange for a full pot of milk.

After the holiday we got back on the train, and all night I sat on its floor and held Dalia close, praying for her recovery.

After much wandering, we finally reached the port of Burgas in Bulgaria and boarded the "Ma'apilim"[50] ship, which was initially named "Paduca," but during its crossing was renamed "Geulah" ("Redemption"). The captain of the ship was Moka Limon, and 1,388 passengers sailed with us.

---

49 *Kol Nidre* ("All Vows"): The opening prayer on the eve of the Day of Atonement.

50 *Ma'apilim* ("those who are ascending"): The term for Jews who tried to immigrate to Palestine under the British Mandate in violation of British restrictions on immigration.

We boarded the ship on Friday and sailed for seven days, during which we celebrated the holiday of Succot[51]. When we reached the coast of Israel, five British destroyers surrounded us, and one of them rammed our ship. They informed us that we wouldn't be disembarking, but rather sent to detainment in Cyprus.

We began to cry. We didn't understand why they were suddenly stopping us, after everything we had been through. British soldiers boarded the ship. The Haganah[52] leaders begged them to let us enter, but the British hardened their hearts and left us on the ship all night. The shore was right in front of us; we could see Mt. Carmel and the buildings of the city of Haifa, but we couldn't enter the Land of Israel.

Haifa residents sent us grapes and oranges. It was the first time we had ever seen such a fruit, and we called it a "little orange."

The next day the British loaded us onto an English ship and took us to Cyprus. When we reached the island, the British boarded the ship and handed out chocolates. Most of the Jews on the ship said to each other, "Throw their chocolate back in their faces," but I said to Shalom, "Take the chocolate and quietly put it in my pocket. I need it for our baby."

51　*Succot* ("booths"): A week-long holiday during which Jews leave their homes to live in temporary booths, commemorating the booths used by the Children of Israel in the desert.

52　*Haganah* ("defense"): The main paramilitary organization of the Jewish population in Palestine under the British Mandate, until it became the core of the Israel Defense Forces upon the founding of the state.

We reached the camp at Cyprus during the intermediate days of the Succot holiday. The moment I saw the fence surrounding the camp, I was shocked. I couldn't believe that we were again being brought into a camp surrounded by fences. But when we realized that the fences were not electrified, we began to calm down a little and understand that they were not trying to kill us. At the entrance to the camp they took all our documents, as well as all the pictures that we had brought from home. To our great sorrow, we never saw those pictures again. Perhaps the British thought that the photographs were secret information we were smuggling in, but in fact they were just the pictures left of our dear ones who had perished in the Holocaust, and no one can ever compensate us for the loss of those photographs.

We were taken into a tent with bare earth for a floor. I had no idea how to lay the baby down to sleep on the dirt. We were utterly helpless. Later they brought folding camp beds into each tent, and together we fixed up beds for us and for the baby.

We stayed in the camp on Cyprus for three months. When we first arrived, we had no idea how to set ourselves up there, being the first group to arrive at that camp. We turned one tent into a synagogue; they gave us a Torah scroll, and we got ready to celebrate the holiday of Simchat Torah[53] there. One tent was set up as a dining hall, where Israelis, apparently Haganah members, awaited us. They prepared meals for us for the upcoming holiday and the Sabbath. We ate a meal in the dining

---

53   *Simchat Torah* ("Rejoicing in the Torah"): A holiday in which Jews dance with the Torah scroll to celebrate completion of the yearly reading cycle of weekly portions and starting to read again from the beginning (the creation of the world).

room and relaxed a little.

After Succot, we were told to pour 10 buckets of water on the dirt floor of the tent to harden the earth. We did so with the help of a pipe that brought sea water into the camp. We washed the dirt floor of the tent and also bathed.

Shalom collected children around him and began to teach them Hebrew every morning. He and a few other comrades brought pieces of wood and together built a table and benches where he would teach the children.

We ate three meals a day in the dining hall. In our remaining free time we walked the length and breadth of the camp. Johnny, one of the British soldiers, befriended us and said that in England he had a daughter Dalia's age. He played with Dalia through the fence and stroked her head, tears in his eyes. I felt sorry for him that he was missing his children in England.

Winter arrived, and rain lashed the tents of the camp. But we, who had survived much worse days, knew that our stay in Cyprus was temporary, the last barrier to be overcome before we reached the Promised Land. The day would come that we would be permitted to enter the Land of Israel.

A few weeks later they transferred us to huts within the camp, and one day they notified us, "Tomorrow we're going to the Land of Israel!"

Excited and happy, we traveled to the port, where we boarded a British ship. One of the objects we brought along with us was an aluminum washtub called a "*paila*," made for us at the Cyprus camp by a Jewish metalworker who had been detained with us and had fashioned various implements from large food cans. Dalia loved to sit in it.

Of the several-hour sea journey, one of the most exciting moments was when we sang "Hatikva" together as one, with pounding hearts and tears in our eyes. At the end of the trip, we left the ship in the Haifa port and, for the first time, stepped on the soil of the Land of Israel. It was three days after Tu b'Shvat[54] in the Jewish year 5708, the end of January 1948.

We kissed the ground and cried over the fact that members of our families had not survived or had the privilege of emigrating to Israel with us. I looked around me at the scenery of the beautiful land we had reached. The air was clear and pure – the air of the Land of Israel. I took a deep breath, filled my lungs with it, and wiped the tears from my eyes.

I had fulfilled my father's last wish. Together with my family, I had reached the Land of Israel!

---

54   *Tu b'Shvat* (15th of the month of Shvat): A holiday marking the New Year of Trees, when trees and plants in Israel begin to blossom after the winter rains.

Do not Forgive

It is harder for me to stay silent than to speak,
Therefore I began to tell the story,
There is a thundering silence – which causes damage and
pain,
And there is a silence that is covered in blood.
I am now returning from Poland,
The cursed earth soaked with Jewish blood.
I begged for revenge, yes, I begged for it and sought it.
This time I truly met it and found it.
I traveled with a mission of two hundred young people.
They are good, beautiful, and successful, and thanks to them,
I am saved.
They became my grandchildren,
The adults on the mission became my friends.
We tied a knot of a promise – that you will carry on for me.
Tell the stories, remember, and don't let people forget.
And do not forgive
The suffering of the Jewish people, caused
By the Germans and the Poles and other people, by force.
May it be God's will that there will never be another Holo-
caust like this to the Jewish people,
Because today we have the spirit, the power, and the brains.

Israel, you are blessed that these are your children.
We are the victory and the revenge against your enemies.
We will guard you like the apple of our eye,
And pray for you for the complete redemption.

We Returned to Visit Auschwitz-Birkenau

After a long time, years,
I came to Auschwitz-Birkenau again.
This time I am the hero;
I come with several of my successful family, may God grant
them long life.
The place is different, there are trees, greenery, and lawns.
Nature has changed the look of the huts: the rain, the frost,
and the rust.
The teeth of time have nibbled at them and made them
crippled.
But I saw: smoke, fire, I smelled a terrible stench.
In my mind's eye I saw masses of emaciated people,
Standing by the fences, in striped uniforms and pale faces.
A few, perhaps, recognized me.
They could recognize that I, too, had been here,
They nodded their heads and encouraged me, "Tell more, tell
more,
Because the world does not yet believe."
But I am backed up by my successful family, praise God,
And other Jews from the whole world.
We will not let the world forget.
We will fight those who deny and those who do not
understand.
We will remind them, you sinned. You committed crimes.

You murdered.
You set on fire. You burned. You took. You tortured.
We will say to the world: "Never again!"
From me, one who was here at the age of sixteen,
One girl in Auschwitz.

8th of the month of Elul, 5772 (August 26, 2012)

IN MEMORIAM

The book is dedicated to the memory of Shalom Leibovits, may his memory be blessed, my beloved husband and our beloved father, who took in that 16-year-old girl from Auschwitz and raised a wonderful family with her.

In memory of all our family members, may God avenge their blood, who perished in the Holocaust. We wrote this book to make your voices heard and ensure that they never fall silent.

Levi Yitzhak Leibovits	Blima Hershkovits
Sheindl Leibovits	Rachel Hershkovits
Shmuel Chaim Leibovits	Eliezer Hershkovits
Blima Leibovits	Yosef-Shalom Hershkovits
Shmayahu Leibovits	Faige Hershkovits
Elazar Michael Yehuda Leibovits	Azriel-Tzvi Hershkovits
David Leibovits	Menachem Mendel Elboim
Alexander Zindel Leibovits	Zeindel Elboim
Bila Leibovits	Shlomo Elboim
Esther (Etu) Leibovits	Rachel Beila Elboim
Gittel (Gitu) Leibovits	Chaim Elboim
Yehuda Leibovits	Moshe Elboim
Golde Leibovits	Chana Elboim
Yakov Hershkovits	Mali Elboim

ACKNOWLEDGMENTS

Thank you to our dear family members, who were with us during the writing of the book: Dalia and Aharon Zitner, Dorit and Tzvika Neuman, Tami Arieli, Revital Arieli, Irit and Itzik Perlmutter, Chedvah and Tzachi Hermeti, Yael and Tzvika Hermeti, Rinat and Nitzachon Azani, Hadas and Yaki Neuman, Re'ut and Yedi'ah Caspi, Yifat and Idan Elor. To Shlomi Elboim, who accompanies, supports, and encourages. To Michael, No'am, Tzuk, Oriah, Yarom, and Ofri Elboim.

Thank you to the people at the Shem Olam Institute in Kfar Haroeh: Rabbi Avraham Kreeger, Rabbi Tzvi Vilner, Rabbi Moshe Chaba and Orit Chermon, for their dedication and investment in the "Emissaries of Memory" course, for their guidance on second-generation Holocaust survivors giving testimony, and for their guidance towards evidence of Jews' acts of kindness to each other during the Holocaust. To Orit Chermon for her guidance on planning the chapters of the book. To Professor Gid'on Greif for his expertise on the subject of Auschwitz and his clarification of terms, dates, and events in Auschwitz. To Dr. Tzvi Moses for his guidance. A big thanks to the members of the first "Emissaries of Memory" course, who became not only dear friends, but also brothers and sisters:

Rivki Ohana, Esther Orenbuch, Ze'ev Atra, Sarah Bazak, Esther Gutman, Shlomit Gelman, Gita Geller, David Zilberberg, Rachel Chalamish, Shlomo Taub, Miriam Levine, Rabbi Motti Sandovsky, Ilan Kalman, and Mina Shtern. Thank you to each one of you for the light that you added to the writing of this book. Special thanks to Gita Geller, whose book "From You and to You, Mother" (Hebrew) was a model and inspiration for writing this book.

Thank you to Dr. Miriam David who enabled the two of us to go on the youth mission to Poland in the Jewish year 5774 (2014). Thank you also to the members of the mission from the schools: Kiryat Chinuch Netivei No'am Darcha, Gadera; Levinson High School, Kiryat Yam; and Meitarim School, Ra'anana. Your desire to hear the testimony added greatly to our desire to make it heard and document it in a book.

To Israel Alter from Ganzach Kiddush Hashem in Bnei Brak for keeping the garment from Auschwitz on display.

To Yad vaShem for locating the testimony of Sara Leibovits from August 1996.

To the Auschwitz-Birkenau Museum in Poland for locating the information on Sara Leibovits.

To Roberta Solit, director of the Veliki Komyati site, for finding documents and information on residents of the village of Komjat, including details on the Hershkovits family.

To Talia Chasin and Gadi Eidelheit for their important comments and clarifications. To Ilana Eidelheit for her assistance in translating the song from German.

Thank you to the people at Yedioth Ahronoth Publishing: to Dovi Eichenwald, who opened the door to memorialization of the Holocaust testimonies, to the devoted Batya Bodner, to Ofra Gelbert-Avni, the wonderful, diligent editor, and to Rotem Kislev, the wonderful language editor.

With much gratitude to all the good people we met along the way. Together we will add light and goodness to the world!

Sara Leibovits and Eti Elboim, first- and second-generation survivors of the Holocaust and heroines dedicated to the resurrection of Israel.

Made in the USA
Monee, IL
21 October 2022